CUSTOMER SERVICE TRAINING 101

CUSTOMER SERVICE SERVICE TRAINING 101

Quick and Easy Techniques That Get Great Results

Renée Evenson

AMACOM

American Management Association

New York | Atlanta | Brussels | Chicago | Mexico City | San Francisco
Shanghai | Tokyo | Toronto | Washington, D. C.

Special discounts on bulk quantities of AMACOM books are available to corporations, professional associations, and other organizations. For details, contact Special Sales Department, AMACOM, a division of American Management Association, 1601 Broadway, New York, NY 10019.

Tel.: 212–903–8316. Fax: 212–903–8083.

Web site: www. amacombooks.org

This publication is designed to provide accurate and authoritative information in regard to the subject matter covered. It is sold with the understanding that the publisher is not engaged in rendering legal, accounting, or other professional service. If legal advice or other expert assistance is required, the services of a competent professional person should be sought.

Library of Congress Cataloging-in-Publication Data

Evenson, Renée, 1951–
    Customer service training 101 : quick and easy techniques that
get great results / Renée Evenson.
      p. cm.
    Includes index.
    ISBN 0-8144-7290-7
    1. Customer services. 2. Customer relations. 3. Employees—
Training of. I. Title.
    HF5415.5.E89   2005
    658.8′12—dc22   2005010446

Printing number

10 9 8 7 6 5 4 3 2 1

Contents

Acknowledgments ix

Introduction 1

Tips for the Trainer 3

Tips for the Student 11

PART I Putting Your Best Face Forward

CHAPTER I Taking Baby Steps: The Basics 21

    STEP 1: First Impressions Matter 26

    STEP 2: Courtesy Counts 28

    STEP 3: Attitude Is Everything 30

    STEP 4: Doing the Right Thing: Ethical Issues 33

    Key Points 37

    Practice Lesson 38

    Think About 39

    Quick Quotes 41

CHAPTER 2 Tossing the Ball Back and Forth:
Effective Communication 43

    STEP 1: Saying What You Mean and Meaning
            What You Say 48

    STEP 2: What You Don't Say: Nonverbal
            Communication 50

    STEP 3: Putting Words Together: Grammar Usage 52

    STEP 4: Asking the Correct Questions and Answering
            the Questions Correctly 54

STEP 5: When the Customer Says No 58

STEP 6: Listening Actively 60

Key Points 63

Practice Lesson 65

Think About 67

Quick Quotes 69

CHAPTER 3 **Jumping in with Both Feet:**
Relationship Building 71

STEP 1: Establishing Rapport 78

STEP 2: Interacting Positively with Customers 81

STEP 3: Identifying Customers' Needs 83

STEP 4: Making the Customer Feel Valued 85

STEP 5: Maintaining Ongoing Relationships 87

STEP 6: Different Strokes: Handling Different
Types of Customers 89

Key Points 94

Practice Lesson 96

Think About 99

Quick Quotes 100

PART II **Putting Your Customers First**

CHAPTER 4 **Seeing Eye to Eye: Face-to-Face**
Contacts 103

STEP 1: Saying Hello: Greeting the Customer 109

STEP 2: Between Hello and Goodbye:
Helping the Customer 111

STEP 3: Saying Goodbye: Ending the Interaction 113

Key Points 117

Practice Lesson 118

Think About 119

Quick Quotes 120

CHAPTER 5 **Saying It with a Smile:**
Telephone Contacts 121

STEP 1: Putting Your Best Ear Forward 126

STEP 2: Saying Hello: The Opener 128

STEP 3: Between Hello and Goodbye:
Helping the Customer 130

STEP 4: Saying Goodbye: The Closer 134

Key Points 137

Practice Lesson 138

Think About 140

Quick Quotes 141

CHAPTER 6 **Looking Before You Leap:**
E-commerce Contacts 143

STEP 1: What Does the E-customer Expect? 147

STEP 2: Hanging the Open Sign: Being Accessible 149

STEP 3: Writing What You Mean:
E-mail Communication 151

STEP 4: Speaking Around the World:
Cross-Cultural Etiquette 154

Key Points 155

Practice Lesson 156

Think About 158

Quick Quotes 159

CHAPTER 7 **Calming the Storm:**
Difficult Customer Contacts 161

STEP 1: What Is Going on: Determine
the Reason 167

STEP 2: What Caused It: Identify the Root Cause
of the Problem 170

STEP 3: What Can I Do: Rectify the Situation 173

STEP 4: What Can I Say: Acknowledge
the Problem 176

STEP 5: What Needs to Be Done: Fix What Needs
to Be Fixed 179

Key Points 183

Practice Lesson 184

Think About 187

Quick Quotes 188

PART III Putting It All Together

CHAPTER 8 Hitting the Ground Running: Ready, Set, Go

CHAPTER 8 **Hitting the Ground Running:
Ready, Set, Go** 191

CHAPTER 9 Being the Best You Can Be: The Total Package

CHAPTER 9 **Being the Best You Can Be:
The Total Package** 197

Quick Quotes 200

Index 203

Acknowledgments

My thanks to . . .

My agent, Michael Snell, for believing in me and for being my toughest critic. Your advice was always on target and helped me become a better writer.

My editor, Ellen Kadin, who supported me throughout this process. I greatly appreciate your positive and helpful attitude.

My illustrator, Susan Pribish, Teleset Company, Hillsborough, New Jersey. You understood what I wanted even when I didn't quite know how to communicate it.

My graphics designer, Stephanie Ward, Teleset Company. You are always ready when I need you, even when I have tight deadlines.

My proofreaders, Rose Aschbrenner, Joseph Balka, and Sarah Randolph. You were my extra eyes and told me what needed to be fixed.

My brother, Don Aschbrenner, for helping me with the training tips. Your expertise in this area helped me tremendously.

My sister, Sharon, for helping me brainstorm ideas. You have always been there for me.

My clients, who asked for this. You gave me the incentive to write this book.

My family and friends. A special thanks for your support.

I am deeply grateful for each and every one of you.

Renée Evenson

CUSTOMER SERVICE TRAINING 101

Introduction

With so much competition in today's global economy, providing exceptional customer service is no longer an added benefit; it is a necessity. *Customers who are not satisfied with the way they are treated can easily take their business elsewhere.*

Whether your business is a multimillion dollar enterprise or a one-person operation, customers pay attention to how they are treated. They are buying more than your product. Consumers will often pay more, drive farther, and inconvenience themselves to do business with a company that appreciates them. Providing exceptional service will build the bond that keeps customers coming back time and time again. Customers may first come into your business because of your product, but they will decide to come again based on how well they are treated. If they are not treated properly, they will go elsewhere.

Providing exceptional customer service is accomplished by positively interacting with customers through effective communication and relationship building. Learning how to treat your customers exceptionally well will bring about an unexpected result: your customers will become a marketing tool for your business. People talk. Whether you provide great customer service or poor customer service, the people with whom you do business are going to tell others how they are treated. When people hear good things about your business, they are more likely to do business with you as well.

Your customers will benefit from this training. They will come away from their transaction with your business feeling they have been treated exceptionally well. They will feel they have been treated fairly and professionally. Most importantly, they will feel that you and your employees appreciate them.

Your employees will benefit from this training. They will take more responsibility for their customers and for their work. They will care more about their jobs and about their company. They will gain more job satisfaction and feel good about coming to work. Absenteeism and turnover may even be reduced.

You will benefit from this training. After you and your employees complete this training, you will become more focused. Your employees will know how to handle a variety of situations to your customers' and your company's satisfaction. You will not have to devote valuable time to handling customer problems. When you train your employees to effectively do their jobs, you will be free to effectively do yours.

Your entire organization will benefit from this training. You will achieve increased efficiency and effectiveness. You and your employees will develop a sense of cooperation, caring, teamwork, and cohesiveness. You will see improved morale, loyalty, and commitment to your customers and to your business.

However, customer service training will only go so far. Your employees must also know *how* to handle your customers' *requests.* Before beginning this training, make sure your employees understand their job duties. Make sure they know how far they can go when trying to satisfy customers. Specific methods and procedures that apply to your business should be taught and clearly understood before beginning these lessons. Doing so will make it easier and also more logical for your employees to incorporate these customer service techniques into their daily routine. Doing so will enable your employees to provide an exceptional experience for each customer.

Why is this book important? The answer is simple: Providing great customer service costs much less, in dollars and *sense,* than providing poor service. It costs more to gain new customers than it does to maintain existing ones. Customers will be more loyal to your business when you treat them well. Simply put, a satisfied customer is more likely to maintain an ongoing business relationship than a dissatisfied customer.

Finally, the most important benefit of customer service training is increased productivity, efficiency, and effectiveness. It is cheaper and faster to do the job right the first time. Satisfying an unhappy customer costs a lot more, both in dollars and cents, than satisfying a customer on the first try.

Tips for the Trainer

TRAINING SESSIONS SHOULD BE A POSITIVE EXPERIENCE FOR BOTH THE TRAINER AND THE TRAINEE.

Training, even if you have never done it before, can be a fun and positive experience for both you and your employees. The key to holding a successful training session lies in preparation. Preparing before you begin will help you feel comfortable and confident and will take the guesswork out of what to expect. Preparation includes identifying your training needs, defining learning outcomes, planning your teaching method, establishing time frames for training sessions, preparing yourself for the training, setting up the room, and following up after the training.

Identify Your Training Needs

To identify your training needs, answer this question: Why did you decide to conduct customer service training? Your immediate response might be "because we need it," but to answer this question reflectively you must first analyze and identify what needs to be improved from both your business and your employees' perspectives.

Think about your business. Make a list of your customer service training needs as they specifically relate to the type of work you do and what your customers expect from you. If you have trouble identifying them, read through each chapter of the book; as you read, relate the material to your customer situations. For example, when reading the chapter on telephone contacts, you may have the "ah-ha" moment when you realize that your employees answer the phone in a non-professional manner.

Next, focus on your employees' needs. Make a customer service learning outcome list for each employee and note strengths, areas of improvement, additional technical or job skills training needed, and any behavioral issues (such as a poor attitude toward customers) that need to be addressed.

After completing the lists, you will be able to . . .

Define Learning Outcomes

Review the needs you identified and develop a list of realistic learning outcomes. What skills should all of your employees demonstrate at the end of the training session? You might want to identify learning outcomes by making a list of each chapter title and writing down the skills in which your employees should be proficient after they complete the training sessions.

Using the example of employees answering calls in a nonprofessional manner, one learning outcome for that chapter could be: *Answer the telephone as ABC Company, then (employee's first name).* Listing specific outcomes before you begin training will enable you to measure how well your employees are using their new skills.

If you identified behavioral issues, you may want to make a separate list for those employees. This will help you focus on those items throughout the training sessions and follow up afterward.

Now that you have identified your learning outcomes, you will be able to . . .

Plan Your Teaching Method

Instructing a group of employees is beneficial both for you and your employees because you can have immediate discussions to clear up problem areas. Training employees self-paced can be beneficial because your employees can work through the material at their own pace, uninterrupted. If you choose self-paced training sessions, follow up with group discussion meetings to make sure everyone has the same understanding of the learning outcomes.

Some suggestions for instructor-led training are:

→ Vary your delivery by reading out loud to the students, having them take turns reading out loud and also reading to themselves.

→ After reading the material, follow up with group discussions related to your business.

→ Hold group brainstorming sessions to solve problems. Ask a question, and note all ideas and suggestions on a flip chart. Discuss which ones will work for your business.

→ For some chapters, divide the group into pairs. Assign a customer service related problem that needs to be solved to each pair. Specify a time period to come up with a solution. Each pair will then present the problem and their solution to the group.

→ Divide the group into role-play pairs. Give each pair a customer service scenario and some additional details to help them get into their roles. For example, for one pair, the customer is upset with your company, and the employee has a condescending attitude; for another, the employee does not listen well. Have one student play the role of the customer and another play the customer service employee. First have them role-play the contact doing it incorrectly, and then again using the correct skills they are learning.

→ To energize the class, play a game related to the material. For example, after completing a session, have the group close their books and call out the key points for the chapter they just completed.

Some suggestions for self-paced training sessions are:

→ Before beginning, briefly review the book with your employees. Explain how you want them to work through the material.

→ If they are to work through the entire book, tell them to check with you periodically (after each part or chapter, for instance).

→ Let them know what to do if they have questions.

→ Explain how you are going to handle the brainstorm topics.

→ Tell them to write down any items they want to discuss in a group meeting.

→ Check on the employees periodically.

→ Plan on meeting with the employees—either group or individually—on completion to review the material and practice lessons.

Before you begin, write an introduction to kick off the training. Make your introduction short and stick to the basics. When you meet with your employees explain why you are conducting this training and discuss the learning outcomes. Keep in mind that you will have everyone's undivided attention—during the first few minutes of speaking! Use this to your advantage and develop a strong introduction. Whether you tell a story, ask a question, or begin with a warm-up exercise or game, make sure these first few minutes grab your employees' attention. Also discuss house-keeping items such as breaks and whether they can have food or a beverage in class.

After planning the training and writing your introduction, you are ready to . . .

Establish Time Frames for Training Sessions

Now that you have reviewed the training material and planned your teaching method, you can establish time frames. What will be the most cost effective and efficient means to conduct the training?

Think about your hours of operation, busy periods, and employee coverage. You already know whether you are going to lead the training class, schedule your employees to work through the training in a self-paced manner, or combine the two methods. Decide whether to work through the entire book in one session or to cover the material in multiple sessions.

Read through the book again, noting the amount of time it takes you to completely work through each chapter. When scheduling your employees, add a little extra time to your estimate to make sure your employees will not feel rushed.

Write a schedule to which you can conform. You will lose credibility with your employees if you schedule a class and then cancel. Give this training priority. If it is important to you, it will be important to your employees.

Once you have established your time frames, you will be able to further . . .

Prepare Yourself for the Training

When you train, establish an open and relaxed atmosphere that encourages discussion by maintaining a positive attitude, keeping focused, remaining neutral, staying relaxed, encouraging everyone to participate, and focusing on the end goals.

Rehearse and practice your presentations—both the general introduction and how you plan to handle each chapter. It is perfectly normal to feel nervous, particularly if training is not part of your routine responsibilities. Being well prepared will help manage your nerves. Practice may not make perfect, but it will help you gain confidence and feel more assured. Here are some tips for training others:

➜ Focus on your students rather than on yourself.

➜ Keep in mind the importance of the material.

➜ Stay on track by making good notes—and using them.

➜ Try to stick to the allotted time, but be sure you plan enough time to be thorough. Do not rush against a time clock. It is better to adjust the time than the material.

➜ When you speak, make eye contact with your students, switching your gaze from one person to another in a pace that is comfortable, not staged.

➜ Vary your voice tone and inflection.

➜ Be yourself. Act naturally.

➜ If you become nervous, take slow, deep breaths to calm yourself.

You are almost ready to begin the training. The last thing to do is . . .

Set Up the Room

Plan a setting conducive to training. First, find a suitable room or area that is free from distractions and noise.

If you are training a group, a U-shaped, rectangle, or round table works well. This way all the students can face each other for discussions, and you will be able to move easily within and around the group. If you will be using an easel or chalkboard, make sure that all students can see it.

If you are conducting individual training, find a quiet place where the student can work at a desk or table. If the training is self-paced, check on the employee frequently to answer questions.

Whether you train a group or your employees work on their own, think of ways to energize them. Look for signs of tiredness or boredom—yawning, fidgeting, or a glazed-over look. Here are some tips for energizing your group:

→ Schedule short breaks every hour or two.

→ Take stretch breaks.

→ If you provide food for class, choose high-energy foods like nuts, raisins, and fruit juices.

→ Pass out a piece of candy for a quick afternoon pick-me-up.

→ Vary the class activities.

→ Hold frequent discussions to break things up.

Now, let the training begin. Make this a positive and fun experience. When you have completed the training sessions, your job is not quite through. To guarantee training success, it is imperative that you . . .

Follow Up After the Training

Spend time with your employees to observe their customer contacts. Try to catch them "doing it right". When they do, acknowledge good performance by giving feedback that is specific to the behavior you observed. Rather than saying, *"you did a great job,"* be more specific by saying, *"I really liked the way you handled Mrs. Johnson when she was upset. The way you explained our delivery schedule was right on target and you made sure she understood completely. Great job."* Now your employee knows exactly what was done right, and the behavior is more apt to be repeated.

It can be a great motivator to praise an employee in earshot of other employees, but it is never acceptable to discuss poor performance in public. When you hear an employee handling a customer poorly, take that employee aside to discuss the incident.

Recognize your group's efforts by commending them, by awarding total team efforts, and by reading customer commendations at meetings.

Most importantly, be consistent with your team. Recognizing good behavior yesterday but ignoring it today will confuse your employees. Make sure customer service is important to you every day; then it will be important to your employees every day, as well.

TRAINING NEEDS

_____

_____

_____

_____

_____

_____

_____

_____

_____

_____

_____

_____

_____

_____

_____

_____

_____

_____

_____

_____

_____

LEARNING OUTCOMES

_____

_____

_____

_____

_____

_____

_____

_____

_____

_____

_____

_____

_____

_____

_____

_____

_____

_____

_____

_____

_____

_____

_____

_____

_____

_____

_____

_____

_____

_____

_____

_____

_____

Tips for the Student

Why is customer service training important? The answer is simple: treating your customers well is essential to your company and to your job. Learning how to give exceptional customer service is necessary for any business to succeed.

What can happen if customer service is not important to a business?

 **PICTURE THIS**

Kris begins a new job working in a gift shop. She enjoys stocking shelves and arranging merchandise in the display cases and window. She gets along well with the other employees. At work, she and her coworkers joke around and have a good time. They have an inside joke about their customers: it would be nice if customers did not bother them. When a customer comes in, they busy themselves with their "real work," ignoring the customer until they are asked for help, then making jokes about who got stuck handling the customer.

After Kris has been working in the shop a few months, she notices that fewer customers are coming in now than when she first started. Business is dropping off. The employees comment that they are happy to have more time to stock shelves without the annoying interference of customers. They also enjoy the relaxed atmosphere and have more time to joke around.

One day their manager has a meeting. She tells the employees that she cannot understand why their sales have been declining, but without sufficient sales revenue she cannot afford to keep the shop open. Kris and the other employees are let go.

Kris is upset. She liked working in the gift shop because it was so much fun. Kris is upset for the wrong reason. She does not understand the most important rule of working in the customer service field: it is the customers, not the company, who pay the wages.

CUSTOMERS = REVENUE = WAGES = EMPLOYEES

Customer service training is important because customers have many choices. If they are not happy with the way they are treated, they can take their business elsewhere, just like the customers in the scenario above.

CUSTOMERS ARE THE REASON YOU HAVE A JOB.

If Kris and her coworkers had learned this simple principle, they would have treated their customers differently.

 **PICTURE THIS**

Kris begins a new job working in a gift shop. On her first day, her manager trains Kris on her job duties, which include stocking shelves and arranging merchandise in the display cases and window. Her most important job, her manager stresses, is to help customers when they come in. No matter what Kris is doing, when a customer comes in, she is to focus her attention on helping that customer. Her manager specifically explains the procedures and expectations for helping customers from the time they walk into the shop until the time they leave.

Kris enjoys stocking shelves and arranging merchandise in the display cases and window. She gets along well with the other employees. At work, she and her coworkers joke around and have a good time. When customers come in, they are given top priority, no matter what the employees are doing. Because the manager explained the importance of customers, Kris and her coworkers understand that their customers are the reason they have jobs.

The manager holds weekly group meetings. She keeps the group up to date on sales revenue data, consistently discusses the importance of customers, and rewards exceptional behavior.

Kris enjoys working in the relaxed atmosphere, where everyone works to achieve the clearly stated company goals. Kris finds tremendous job satisfaction working in the gift shop.

Finally, customer service training is important because your customers are important. Without customers, customer service employees are not needed.

As you work through this training, you will learn how to handle different types of customers in different situations. Taking the time to prepare for your training sessions will help you make the most of the material. Preparation includes identifying your personal needs and defining learning outcomes, getting ready for training sessions, working through the book, and following up after training.

Identify Your Personal Needs and Define Learning Outcomes

Think about your typical customer contacts. Which types of customers or customer interactions are you uncomfortable handling? For example, are you unsure how to talk to customers who are upset and confront you in an angry tone? Make a list of any areas in which you need improvement or guidance.

Now, think about your job from a technical standpoint. What must you learn to do your job effectively? Make a list of those areas in which you need additional training. Before you begin your customer service training, give this list to your manager and ask for technical training first. You need to feel comfortable with your job duties before you can feel comfortable helping your customers.

Finally, think about what you want to gain from training. Make a list of learning outcomes. Turn your areas of improvement into learning outcomes by rephrasing them as positive statements. For example, not knowing how to deal with customers who are angry could be written as a learning objective: *turn irate customers into satisfied ones.*

Get Ready for the Training Session

Being in a training class means being in a different routine. When you are used to interacting with customers, staying alert when you sit, read, and work through a book can be difficult. Make the most of the training sessions by:

→ Getting enough sleep the night before training

→ Eating a healthy breakfast

→ Knowing what to expect during the class

→ Taking deep breaths when you feel drowsy

→ Standing and stretching when you feel sleepy

→ Taking a short walking break when you feel ready to nod off

Work Through the Book

As you work through each chapter, relate what you are reading to the type of customer interactions you have. You and your manager may decide to focus on a specific customer scenario for each chapter. If you do, use the blank pages found in Part II to write down a typical customer request. You can refer to this scenario when answering the practice lesson questions and refer to your answers in group discussions.

Each chapter follows a similar format:

→ General chapter information

→ Scenario handled in a less than satisfactory manner

→ Overview of the key points that will be covered in the chapter

→ Each key point is explained step-by-step in an in-depth manner, with a retake of a portion of the scenario

→ Scenario handled correctly

→ Summary of key points and steps

→ Interactive training lesson

→ Quick quotations for memory joggers

In addition, each chapter contains handy tips and topics for group meeting brainstorming sessions.

Read through a chapter. Review the key points and steps. If you feel comfortable with the material, work the practice lesson. If not, reread the chapter. Make sure you understand the material before moving on to the next chapter. Write down any questions you want to ask your manager or bring up in a group meeting.

Follow Up After Training

Review the learning outcomes you listed before you began. Did you learn how to handle each one? If not, review the relevant chapters again. If, after reading through the material a second time, you still feel uncomfortable or unsure, let your manager know. Your manager can work with you to turn this area of improvement into a strength.

Review your list of questions with your manager. Discuss answers and solutions.

Finally, enjoy your job. Your customers depend on you to be your best.

AREAS OF IMPROVEMENT

ADDITIONAL TECHNICAL TRAINING NEEDED

LEARNING OUTCOMES

PART I

Putting Your Best Face Forward

CHAPTER I

Taking Baby Steps: The Basics

**ALWAYS REMEMBER, THE CUSTOMER
IS THE REASON YOU HAVE A JOB.**

What is happening to customer service? More often than not customers are met with boredom, indifference, and even rudeness or condescension. When they are greeted with a friendly smile and a helpful attitude, they are thrilled. They may even tell their friends. They feel grateful when they get good service. Customers should never have to feel grateful for being treated well. Being treated well should be the standard.

Take off your customer service provider hat for a moment and put on your customer hat. Think about your own interactions as a customer. In the past few days, how many times were you a customer? Did you go to the grocery store or run into a convenience store? Go to the mall? How about visits to the post office, doctor's office, bank, dry cleaners, or your child's school? How many times did you eat a meal out? Did you call a company to place an order or ask a question or did you visit a Web site and order products online?

As a customer, you have many choices. How many restaurants are nearby? How many stores are in your mall? How many doctors are in your phone book?

If you are not happy with the service at one business, you have options. You can go somewhere else.

As a customer service employee, remember that your customers also have choices. If they are not happy with the way you treat them, they can go somewhere else.

How you treat your customers does matter. Think again, about your own interactions as a customer. Which ones stand out in your mind? You are likely to remember service that is outstanding or awful. Mediocre service is soon forgotten.

What Kind of Service Do You Give Your Customers?

Ready to begin? We are going to start with the basics because:

THE BASICS ARE THE BASIS OF CUSTOMER SERVICE.

You begin providing customer service the moment a customer comes into your business, calls you on the telephone, or E-mails you. When customers physically walk through your door, they take a mental snapshot of you and your surroundings. Without even thinking, they form a first impression. First impressions are

also formed over the telephone and through online contact. How you speak, how well you listen, the words you choose, and how you write and respond using E-mail contribute to first impressions. If a customer's first impression is favorable, you have laid the foundation for providing great customer service.

If the first impression is not favorable, you will have to dig deeper to build your foundation.

Being courteous promotes a positive first impression. Customers appreciate courteous treatment. As young children, we learned basic courtesies: to say please and thank you; to pay attention and not to interrupt when other people speak; to treat others with respect; to play fairly; to say I'm sorry. As adults, we sometimes forget how important these words and actions are. Courtesy words, phrases, and behaviors contain powerful messages. They show you care.

Your attitude can also foster a positive first impression. Customers appreciate a positive attitude. A great attitude can help overcome a poor first impression. Similarly, a negative attitude can destroy a favorable first impression.

By combining a favorable first impression, courteous treatment, and a positive attitude, you form the basis for a strong customer service foundation. Add effective communication skills, and you will be on your way to building long lasting relationships with your customers. Once you master these customer service basics, learn how to effectively communicate, and develop skills to build strong relationships, you will confidently handle any customer in any situation.

 **PICTURE THIS**

Sally drives to Bob's Electronic Store to look for a new television set. She walks in and spots two employees stocking CDs on a display rack. They are laughing and joking with each other as they work. Neither looks at her. Neither asks if she needs help. She asks if they carry television sets. Without looking up, one of the employees says, "yeah, they're over there," pointing as he answers. She wanders over to the television sets. With so many new types from which to choose, she does not know what she wants. Neither of the employees asks if she needs help. She makes a mental note of the prices, leaves that store and drives to JB Appliances. A friendly young man greets her at the door. He looks directly at her, smiles, and says hello. She explains that she is looking for a new television, but does not know specifically what she wants. He assures her he can help, walks her to that area of the store, describes the different type sets, and takes the time to answer all her questions. She leaves the store with a new television. Even though the sets are priced higher at JB Appliances, Sally does not care. She likes the courteous way she is treated, so they get her business.

What Went Wrong?

Sally did not form a favorable first impression of the employees at Bob's Electronic Store. Neither stopped what they were doing to help her. Neither were courteous. They could have changed her first impression, but they did not project the attitude that they cared about her as a customer. She did not care for the way she was treated, so she left and did business with another store.

How Did the Customer Feel?

How do you think Sally felt as a result of her treatment at Bob's Electronic Store? _____

_____

_____

_____

_____

_____

How do you think Sally felt as a result of her treatment at JB Appliances?

_____

_____

_____

_____

_____

_____

When you work with customers continuously, it is easy to begin taking them for granted. Remember what happened when Kris and her coworkers took their customers for granted? It is crucial that you not take your customers for granted. When you do, you stop caring about how you treat them. Eventually, you may view customers as though they are intruders who take you away from your work. This is the view Bob's employees and Kris and her coworkers projected. When you do not treat your customers well, you may soon have no customers.

Customers, on the other hand, have been conditioned to expect mediocre service. Customers who are given mediocre service will have mediocre attitudes about the business. When customers are valued and treated with courtesy and respect, they are more apt to do repeat business with you. Remember the important lesson you learned as a child: Always treat others the way you want to be treated. Treat others well, and they will treat you well.

Mastering the basics is simple once you learn and practice the four steps below. Then you will begin to build a firm foundation for providing great customer service.

STEP 1: First Impressions Matter
STEP 2: Courtesy Counts
STEP 3: Attitude Is Everything
STEP 4: Doing the Right Thing: Ethical Issues

If Bob's employees treated Sally better, she would have had no reason to drive to JB Appliances. She left because they did not value her as a customer. They did not lay a foundation for giving great customer service.

In answer to the questions above, you may have answered something like this:

How do you think Sally felt as a result of her treatment at Bob's Electronic Store?
   Invisible.
   Her business did not matter to them.

How do you think Sally felt as a result of her treatment at JB Appliances?
   They cared about her as a customer.
   They made her feel valued.

STEP 1: First Impressions Matter

First impressions are mental snapshots you take when you first encounter a person or situation. First impressions include a person's looks and actions, including general grooming and cleanliness, clothing, voice tone, attitude, body language, and posture. These elements, put together, make up your personal style. First impressions do matter. They matter a lot. When people see you for the first time, what is their first impression of you?

When Sally took her mental snapshot at Bob's, it did not develop well. Even if the employees were well dressed, with neat hair, and clean clothes, their lack of courtesy and poor attitudes spoke volumes. When they ignored Sally, they told her loudly and clearly that they did not value her as a customer.

People see you first, hear you second. The first step to making a good first impression is your appearance. When you do not have a nice appearance, you might present an obstacle that blocks your customers from forming a positive first impression. This does not mean you have to sacrifice your personal style to please others, but when you are at work make sure your appearance is fitting for your business. Otherwise you may have to work harder for your customers to get to know the real you.

Wear appropriate clothing for the type of work you do. Wear the type of clothing that fits the personality of your business. If you work in an expensive restaurant, you will dress quite differently than if you work in a fast food restaurant. When in doubt about what type clothing is suitable for your job, always lean toward dressing conservatively. Save your party clothes for parties. Save your torn jeans and old tees for hanging out with friends.

No matter what type of clothes you wear to work, you do not have to spend a fortune on your wardrobe. Wearing well-fitted and appropriate clothes will go a long way toward presenting yourself successfully. It does not matter how much you spend; what matters most is how your clothes fit you and your environment.

Make sure you are groomed. This means your hair and fingernails are clean and neat; your face, body, and teeth are clean; your clothes are clean and pressed;

your shoes are polished; your hair is styled; and your overall image is professional. Put all that together, and you present a groomed look.

 If you do not have a full-length mirror, buy one. Look in it every day before you leave home.

Maintain a relaxed and open demeanor. You can wear nice clothes, be clean and groomed, yet still convey a negative first impression. Your body language counts as much as your grooming. Whether you present an angry, bored, or friendly demeanor, it shows. Hold your head high, and keep your facial expressions friendly. Make eye contact when talking with someone. Smile as often as appropriate; smile often. A smile goes a long way, both personally and interpersonally. When you smile, you feel better. When you smile, you make others feel better.

Doing these three things will help your customers begin forming a positive first impression of you. Doing these three things shows that you care about yourself. What are your customers seeing?

HOW COULD BOB'S EMPLOYEES HAVE MADE A BETTER FIRST IMPRESSION?

Sally drives to Bob's Electronic Store to purchase a new television set. She walks in and spots two employees stocking CDs on a display rack. They are dressed nicely and look happy, as they laugh and joke with each other while they work. They look at her, smile, and say, "Welcome to Bob's."

This time, Sally's photo was developing nicely. The employees were well-groomed, and their body language conveyed the message that they cared about themselves. Their smiles conveyed the message that they cared about her. Sally smiled back and said she was looking for a new television.

STEP 2: Courtesy Counts

Young children are praised for doing and saying the right things. When a young child says *please* and *thank you,* people respond positively. When a young child says *I'm sorry,* people readily accept the apology. When children wait to speak without interrupting, people notice how well mannered they are. When children learn how to play well, people comment. Children who receive positive reinforcement develop valuable skills for getting along with others.

As an adult, you are not going to receive constant praise for being courteous, but people will appreciate your behavior. When you act courteously, you send a positive and powerful message. When you make a conscious effort to use courtesy words and phrases, they will soon become a natural part of your vocabulary and personality.

Say please, thank you, and you're welcome. As a child, you learned to say *please* when asking for something: *Can I please have a glass of water?* You learned to say *please* when you responded to others: *Yes, please.* You learned to say *thank you* when someone did something for you. You learned to say *you're welcome* when someone thanked you for doing something. Make it a habit to incorporate these words into your vocabulary and use them frequently.

Say excuse me and I'm sorry. Growing up you learned that when you did not understand someone, when someone was in your way, or when you inadvertently did something incorrectly, you said *excuse me.* When you did something wrong or made a mistake you learned to say *I'm sorry.* Saying *I'm sorry,* in particular, is difficult for adults. Get in the habit of adding this to your vocabulary. The next time you do something wrong, say *I'm sorry.* Not only will you make the other person feel better, but you will feel better. These two words go a long way in repairing relationship damage.

Use Sir and Ma'am. Using these words shows a sign of respect. When you call a person *sir* or *ma'am,* be careful how you accentuate these words. The wrong emphasis can make you sound sarcastic or condescending. The right emphasis can make you sound respectful.

Use a person's name when you know it. Everyone enjoys hearing his or her name, so if you know your customer's name use it. Also be sure to give the customer your name.

Use yes rather than yeah. *Yes* sounds professional, intelligent, and respectful. Period. Save *yeah* for personal conversations.

Say it with a smile. This is an old saying with a timely meaning. In today's fast-paced world, smiling when you speak *does* come across loud and clear. Whether you are speaking face to face or by telephone, your customers will see or hear the smile in your voice.

There are also things you should not do in the presence of customers. They include talking on a personal call, smoking, eating (or having food at your work station), and chewing gum.

HOW COULD BOB'S EMPLOYEES HAVE INCORPORATED BASIC COURTESIES INTO THEIR CONVERSATION WITH SALLY?

Sally smiles back and says, "I'm looking for a new television, but there are so many new types I really don't know what I'm looking for. Can you help me?"

"Yes Ma'am, my name is Jeff, and I'll be happy to help you," says one of the employees as he smiles warmly and walks toward her. "Let me show you what we have." He walks with her to the television sets.

Jeff was courteous, and his first words made Sally feel he truly cared about helping her.

STEP 3: Attitude Is Everything

People may not remember the color of the shirt you wore or the exact words you said, but they will remember your attitude. Projecting a positive attitude is another way to make a good—and long-lasting—impression on others. **It** really *is* all in the presentation. The **it** factor is the attitude you present to the world.

Attitude is everything. Good *or* bad. Whether yours is good or bad, your attitude is what people are going to remember about you. When you interact with customers, you may not get a second chance. Even if you are not a naturally positive person you can learn to have a more positive attitude. It begins by learning to appreciate.

Appreciate the good in yourself and in others. Appreciation can be learned by changing your self-talk (the words you use when you think) to positive thoughts. This goes for thoughts about yourself: Change *I'll never do this right* to *Next time I'll do better.* This also goes for thoughts about your customers: *Look at this old lady. She doesn't look like she has a clue about television sets. This is going to be a tough one to handle.* Change this mindset to *I'll do what I can to help this customer. She mentioned she doesn't know a whole lot about all the new type sets, so I'll do my best to explain them all.* Changing your self-talk helps you appreciate yourself and others. When you find yourself falling into old habits of negative self-talk, make a conscious effort to change your thought process.

Believe in yourself. When you stop your negative self-talk, you will start to believe in yourself. Saying things such as, *I'll never do this right,* only sets you up for failure. Changing your self-talk to *Next time I'll do it differently* sets you up for success. When you begin to believe in yourself, you will begin to feel more confident. When you feel more confident, you will begin projecting a powerful image to others. To your customers, you will project an image of someone who believes in yourself, your company, and your products.

Believe you can make a difference. When you believe in yourself and gain confidence, you will naturally progress to believing that you can make a difference in the lives of others. When you believe you can make a difference, you will find ways to make it happen. At work, look for ways to make a difference by being helpful, interested, and caring toward your customers.

Keep an open mind; do not stereotype people. When the employee thought about the older woman who did not know what she wanted and was going to be tough to handle, he was accepting a negative stereotype about older people before he talked to her. That older woman might be smarter and sharper than he is. Remember first impressions? Stereotypes can skew first impressions. Do you want people to stereotype you? When you change your thought process and stop stereotyping others, you will change the way you present yourself.

Stress can easily zap anyone's positive attitude. If you find yourself getting stressed at work, try to get away from the situation for a few minutes. Getting away will not only help you calm down, it will help put things in perspective. The best remedy for keeping stress at bay, though, is to take care of *you* every day. Get enough rest. Exercise your body and mind. Eat healthy foods. Do something fun. Do something just for you. When you do these things every day, you will have a better outlook and be able to keep stress at arm's length.

We all carry emotional baggage. When you arrive at work, leave your emotional baggage at the door. Never make your customers and coworkers suffer because you are having a problem. Remember that everyone has problems. Use your work time to let go of personal baggage.

HOW COULD BOB'S EMPLOYEE HAVE SHOWN A POSITIVE ATTITUDE?

As they walk to the television sets, Jeff asks, "Have you been to Bob's before?" When Sally shakes her head, he smiles and continues, "We're glad you decided to come in. Not only do we offer the lowest prices around, we stand behind all our merchandise."

Sally nods. She likes what she is hearing.

When they reach the television display, Jeff says, "I'll tell you about the different type of sets we have and be happy to answer any questions."

Sally completed developing her picture. She liked Jeff's confident, positive attitude. He took the time to answer all her questions and guided her to make the right decision. Sally left Bob's with a new television.

STEP 4: Doing the Right Thing: Ethical Issues

The last step of customer service basics deals with ethics. Being ethical means being honest, doing the right thing, and being accountable for your actions.

Always be honest. Being honest at all times will make your life far less complicated. When you are truthful, you do not have to remember what you said to whom. Being truthful is important to your customers. When you are dishonest, people find out. Maybe not right away, but the truth always has a way of coming out. When people find out you have not been completely honest, they will no longer trust you.

Do the right thing. When you make the decision to always do the right thing for others, you will go out of your way to do your best. At work, when you are faced with a dilemma, base your decision on doing what is right and ethical. Being ethical includes treating all your customers fairly and equally.

One of your customers asks you for a special favor. Doing so will mean crossing the ethical line. How do you tactfully refuse? You could say, *"I don't feel comfortable doing that because it is against our company's policy."* If the customer persists, ask your manager for help.

Do what you say you will when you say you will. Become a person others can rely on. When you give a customer your word, mean it. Let your word be your bond. Erase the words *I can't* and *no* from your vocabulary. If you cannot do what the customer asks, explain instead what you *can do*. It is all right to say *"I don't know."* Follow up with *"I'll find out for you."*

Always be truthful about your products, services, and policies. Never make misleading claims.

Never comment negatively about your competitors. If a customer asks for a comparison or leads you to say something negative, say, *"I don't know about that but let me explain our policy...."* or *"I don't know enough about that to comment."*

Be accountable for your actions. If you think you have done something incorrect or unethical, be up front and talk it over with your manager. When you take responsibility and own up to your mistakes, people will respect you. No one expects you to make the right decision 100% of the time. We are all human and are all going to make mistakes. What sets ethical people apart is that they hold themselves accountable for their mistakes. This may not be easy at first, but it is the right thing to do. People will appreciate that you are able to admit you did something wrong. You will also have an added benefit: You will respect yourself more when you take responsibility for your actions.

HOW COULD BOB'S EMPLOYEE DEAL WITH AN ETHICAL ISSUE?

Sally is ready to buy. She says, "I heard that JB Appliances gives four free DVDs when you purchase a television. I'll buy from you if you give me some DVDs."

How does Jeff handle this? He is not familiar with JB's policy so he should not say, "JB offers that because they sell their televisions at a higher price, and they don't stand behind their merchandise. I've heard complaints about them." Never comment about another company.

Or . . . he might say, "Well, we usually don't do that, but for you I'll make an exception." Never offer a special deal unless you are willing to extend it to all of your customers. Imagine if you do this and Sally tells her friend, who bought a television set from Bob's yesterday. He is not going to be happy that he was not offered the free DVDs.

Now here is what Jeff can say, "I'm not familiar with what JB Appliances offers, but here's what we offer. We always keep our merchandise priced low to consistently give our customers the best deal."

By positively reassuring Sally and explaining their policy, Jeff does not get involved in an ethical dilemma.

What Is Ethical?

Do you know what is considered ethical, and more importantly, unethical, in your business? If you are unclear, discuss specific situations that are unethical. In today's business climate, every employee should be completely certain they know the difference.

When You Unwittingly Do Something Unethical

One of your customers asks you to do something special or unusual, such as waiving a service fee. You willingly comply, but later realize that you crossed ethical boundaries. How do you handle the situation? Do you call the customer and retract the favor? Do you extend the favor to all customers, having done it for one?

Discuss how to handle sticky situations you may encounter. As a group, come up with suggested responses. Role play to reinforce ethical behavior.

PICTURE THIS

Sally drives to Bob's Electronic Store to purchase a new television set. She walks in and spots two employees stocking CDs on a display rack. They are dressed nicely and look happy as they laugh and joke with each other while they work. They look at her, smile, and say, "Welcome to Bob's."

Sally smiles back and says, "I'm looking for a new television, but there are so many new types I really don't know what I'm looking for. Can you help me?"

"Yes Ma'am, my name is Jeff and I'll be happy to help you," says one of the employees as he smiles and walks toward her. "Let me show you what we have." He walks with her to the television sets.

As they walk to the television sets, Jeff asks, "Have you been to Bob's before?" When Sally shakes her head, he smiles and continues, "We're glad you decided to come in. Not only do we offer the lowest prices around, we stand behind all our merchandise."

Sally nods. She likes what she is hearing.

When they reach the television display, Jeff says, "I'll tell you about the different type of sets we have and be happy to answer any questions."

Jeff takes the time to answer all her questions and guides her to make the right decision. Sally leaves Bob's with a new television.

Customer service begins when you are courteous to your customers. It really is that simple.

The Basics
KEY POINTS

STEP 1: First Impressions Matter

People see you first, hear you second

Wear appropriate clothing for the type of work you do

Make sure you are well groomed

Maintain a relaxed and open demeanor

STEP 2: Courtesy Counts

Say *please, thank you,* and *you're welcome*

Say *excuse me* and *I'm sorry*

Use *sir* and *ma'am*

Use a person's name when you know it

Use *yes,* rather than *yeah*

Say it with a smile

STEP 3: Attitude Is Everything

Attitude is everything—good or bad

Appreciate the good in yourself and in others

Believe in yourself

Believe you can make a difference

Keep an open mind; do not stereotype people

STEP 4: Doing the Right Thing: Ethical Issues

Always be honest

Do the right thing

Do what you say you will when you say you will

Be accountable for your actions

The Basics
PRACTICE LESSON

STEP 1: First Impressions Matter

Write down some things you can do to make a good first impression.

_____

_____

_____

_____

STEP 2: Courtesy Counts

Write some statements you can say to your customers that incorporate basic courtesies.

_____

_____

_____

_____

STEP 3: Attitude Is Everything

What are some things you can do to present a great attitude?

_____

_____

_____

_____

STEP 4: Doing the Right Thing: Ethical Issues

Think of a situation in which a customer asks you to do something un-ethical. Briefly describe the situation and your response to the customer.

_____

_____

_____

_____

Think About . . .

Have **you** ever formed a wrong first impression?

Calvin walked into a tire store. He spotted two employees, one on the showroom floor straightening up the displays and another behind the counter keying on a computer. He liked the look of the employee behind the counter, but he did not like the look of the floor employee. Without even thinking about it, Calvin began forming first impressions of both employees.

The employee on the showroom floor looked at Calvin, smiled warmly and said, "Hi, welcome to Westview Tire."

Calvin ignored him and walked to the counter. *No way do I want him helping me,* Calvin thought, *not the way he looks.* He waited for the other employee, who was busy inputting information, to look up. Calvin waited. And waited.

While he was waiting, another customer came in. The floor employee smiled and said, "Hi, welcome to Westview Tire. How can I help you?"

Calvin, continuing to wait, noticed that the employee helping the customer went out of his way to explain the different types of tires. *Actually,* Calvin thought, *maybe I judged him incorrectly. He's doing a great job explaining the different tires.* The employee was knowledgeable and answered all the customer's questions while Calvin continued to wait.

Finally Calvin said, "Excuse me, can you help me?"

Without looking up, the man behind the counter blandly said, "I'll be with you as soon as I'm done."

Meanwhile, the floor employee began writing up the other customer's work order.

Hmm, Calvin thought, *I definitely was wrong about him.* He really is doing a great job helping that person.

The employee looked up from his computer. "OK, I'm done. What do you need?" No smile. No hello.

"That's all right," Calvin said, "I don't want to bother you. I'll wait until he's done."

Calvin learned a valuable lesson about people. He began forming his first impression based on a stereotype he had about the way the floor employee looked, rather than noticing the employee's courteous actions and positive attitude.

On the other hand, perhaps the floor employee did not present a favorable image to foster a positive first impression. Because Calvin formed a negative first impression, the employee had to show him, through his actions, that Calvin was wrong in his opinion. By being courteous and having a helpful attitude, the employee was able to change Calvin's initial impression.

The Basics
QUICK QUOTES

Be helpful and enthusiastic

Do everything with integrity

Keep your facial expressions friendly

Maintain a friendly and open demeanor

Say it with a smile

Use *yes* rather than *yeah*

Always be honest

Never give the customer a reason to lose trust in your company

It is all in your presentation

Attitude is everything—good or bad

CHAPTER 2

Tossing the Ball Back and Forth: Effective Communication

**IN YOUR DEALINGS WITH CUSTOMERS,
BE THE ONE TO INITIATE
HONEST, RESPECTFUL, AND
THOUGHTFUL COMMUNICATION.**

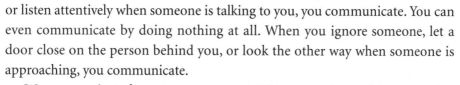

Did you know that almost everything you do in life involves some form of communication? Anytime you interact with another person, you communicate. Whether you smile at a stranger, speak to a friend, or listen attentively when someone is talking to you, you communicate. You can even communicate by doing nothing at all. When you ignore someone, let a door close on the person behind you, or look the other way when someone is approaching, you communicate.

We communicate for numerous reasons. We communicate when we need to make decisions, solve problems, get answers, gather information, or resolve conflicts. We communicate when we want to find out how someone is doing, find out what is happening, discuss important events, or get to know someone. A smile communicates volumes. So does a scowl. Communicating is so important a person's success often depends on good communication skills.

How Well Do You Communicate?

As a front-line employee, you are your customers' point of contact and their primary communication source. To them, you not only represent the company, you **are** the company.

As your company's communicator, how you communicate with your customers is important. In fact, it is your most important job. Relationships develop when effective communication is established. You will learn about building relationships in Chapter 3, but first you will learn valuable communication skills. Communication forms the basis of any relationship; at work, learning how to communicate effectively is imperative when you deal with customers.

The easiest way to communicate is when you are face to face with people. You have the advantage of picking up cues about a person's moods and can adjust your conversation accordingly. You also communicate by telephone and by writing E-mails and letters. You do have an advantage when communicating through E-mail or writing because you can read—and change—what you write before sending it. When speaking face to face, you have no backspace or delete key to change your message. It is crucial in verbal communication that you say exactly what you mean to say. Using good grammar helps communicate the correct message.

Try this verbal communication exercise: Ask the following question out loud in an enthusiastic tone.
"Can I help you?"

Repeat it in:
An unsure tone
An angry tone
A disinterested tone

Notice how the same four words take on four very different meanings, depending on your voice tone. **How** you say something is even more important than the words you choose. How you say something can help—or hinder—the effectiveness of your communication.

Besides verbal communication, you can also communicate without saying a word. When communicating face to face, your body language accounts for a major portion of communication. Nonverbal communication, including your posture, facial expressions, and hand and eye movements are all manners of communicating. You may say one thing, but communicate something else. Words communicate a message; body language communicates the emotions behind the message.

Try this nonverbal communication exercise: Picture yourself explaining a company policy to a customer. As you are speaking:

Look at the person and smile

Slump over and yawn

Lower your eyes to the floor

Stand with your arms folded in front of you

When you look directly at someone and smile, you convey interest. When you slump and yawn, you convey boredom. When you lower your eyes to the floor, you convey disinterest or dishonesty. When you stand with your arms folded in front of you, you build an imaginary wall between you and the other person. You can say the right words, but still convey the wrong message.

It is also important that what you are saying is being interpreted the way you mean it. How many times has someone taken your message the wrong way? When that happens, it takes more of your time and energy to correct the listener's interpretation of your meaning. When you speak, it is important that you choose your words carefully. When you listen, it is equally important that you pay attention to what you hear.

A large part of your communication with customers will be in the form of asking questions. Knowing what questions to ask is crucial, but so is knowing when to ask them. The tone you use when you ask a question is also as important as the words you choose.

PICTURE THIS

Steve stops at the local deli for lunch. He is in a hurry to place the order for himself and his coworkers and is greeted by an employee who yawns as he looks at Steve. Scratching his head with his pencil, he says, "Hey man, whaddyawant?"

"I'm in a hurry. Is it possible to get my order quickly?"

The employee shrugs nonchalantly. "I suppose so. We're not that busy right now."

Steve begins to give his order, "I'll have a turkey and Swiss on whole wheat with mayo and tomatoes. . . ." As he speaks he notices the employee keeps looking at the door whenever someone comes in. Steve finishes his order, "a ham on rye with mustard and a pastrami on rye with mustard."

The employee says, "OK, a ham on rye and a pastrami on rye. What do you want on 'em?"

As Steve says "mustard" he wonders if the employee got the rest of the order. "Did you get the turkey and Swiss, the roast beef, and the tuna salad?"

Without looking up, he says "Yeah" in an agitated voice. The employee strolls slowly to the backroom with Steve's order.

Before Steve leaves, he checks his order because he is not certain the employee got it right.

What Went Wrong?

Steve felt he was talking to himself and that the employee was not listening. The employee looked tired, bored, and was more interested in seeing who was coming in than helping Steve. His choice of words and poor grammar did nothing to help Steve feel confident that the order would be right.

How Did the Customer Feel?

How do you think Steve felt after giving his order?

_____

_____

_____

_____

How did Steve feel about this deli when he left?

_____

_____

_____

_____

Whether you work in a physician's office, a restaurant, a retail store, a professional office, a service station, or a call center, effective communication is always important. When your primary job is to be your company's communicator, you project your company's image to the customers. In this chapter you will learn valuable tools to help you become a more effective communicator. The six steps to effective communication are:

STEP 1: Saying What You Mean and Meaning What You Say
STEP 2: What You Don't Say: Nonverbal Communication
STEP 3: Putting Words Together: Grammar Usage
STEP 4: Asking the Correct Questions and Answering the
          Questions Correctly
STEP 5: When the Customer Says No
STEP 6: Listening Actively

If the deli employee had communicated more effectively, Steve would have had more confidence that his order was correct. Although he was in a hurry to get back to his office, he took the time to check his order before leaving the deli.

You may have answered the questions above something like this:

How do you think Steve felt after giving his order?
    Because the employee paid more attention to who was coming and going, he had no confidence that the employee got the order right.

How did Steve feel about this deli when he left?
    The business owner/manager/employee did not care about him as a customer.
    The owner/manager did not care about the way their employees handled customers.

STEP 1: Saying What You Mean and Meaning What You Say

When you communicate, you can either speak or listen. It is impossible to do both well at the same time. As the speaker, you control the conversation. You have the listener's interest—as long as you are saying something that is receptive. As the speaker, it is your responsibility to get your message across the way you mean it. You may not get a second chance to explain.

Choose the right words. In other words, think before you speak. Choose words that will be understandable to the listener. When you speak to a toddler, you choose words that are understandable for that age level. When you speak to a customer who may not be familiar with your company or products, choosing the right words will help convey the correct message. Opt for easy and familiar words. Trying to impress people with big words may only add confusion to your message.

Make sure your tone fits the message you are sending. How you say something is more important than what you say. When you did the verbal exercise and asked a question four different ways, you got four different meanings. In addition to choosing the right words, think about how you want to say the words. When you talk to someone and use the wrong tone, your message will be misinterpreted. Use a serious, helpful tone when speaking to a customer who is upset. Use an enthusiastic tone when asking a customer if you can help. When asking questions, use a tone that shows you are truly interested in the answer. Pay attention to your listener's nonverbal cues to make sure your tone fits your customer.

Add welcome words to your vocabulary. When you use words that sound positive and confident, you will project a positive and confident attitude. Words and phrases like *Yes!, I'll be happy to!,* and *Sure I can!* send a message to your customers that you really are happy to help them. Words like *definitely* and *absolutely* send a message that you are enthusiastic and interested. It is difficult to say *definitely* without showing conviction and interest. It is difficult to say *absolutely* without showing enthusiasm. Interjecting these and other welcome words into your conversation convey a sense of conviction that you truly want to help.

Keep business conversations professional. When you interact with customers, draw the line between being professional and getting personal. Even though you may establish a friendly rapport, your customer is still your customer. Keep your conversations with your customers on a professional level.

When you are speaking with a customer of a different culture who does not understand what you are saying, speak in the same tone and voice level but choose different words to convey your message. Repeating the same words over and over will most likely frustrate the customer—and you.

HOW COULD THE EMPLOYEE HAVE OPENED THE CONVERSATION DIFFERENTLY?

Steve stops at the local deli for lunch. He is in a hurry to place the order for himself and his coworkers and is greeted by an employee who looks at him, smiles, and enthusiastically says, "Hi, Welcome to Max's Deli. How are you doing?"

"I'm doing great, thanks, but I am in a hurry. Is it possible to get my order quickly?"

"Absolutely. I'll put a rush on it. What can I get you?"

This time the employee chose words that were appropriate and he conveyed enthusiasm in his tone. Adding *absolutely* gave Steve confidence that the employee meant what he said.

STEP 2: What You Don't Say: Nonverbal Communication

How you say something is more important than the words you choose, but what you do when you convey a message is also important. You can choose the right words and use an appropriate tone, but convey an entirely different message through nonverbal communication. In the nonverbal exercise, you used four different mannerisms when you spoke to your customer. You said one thing, but sent four entirely different messages.

Actions speak louder than words. You may have a great attitude and personality, but your actions will leave a lasting impression on your customers. Always be aware of your body language to make sure you are sending the right nonverbal messages.

Smile often. A smile is one of the most powerful messages you can send. A smile translates into any language, to any age group, across any culture. Smile and people will smile back at you. Try it. It does work. Get in the habit of smiling often. When you make it a habit to smile, your smile will look natural, not forced. A forced smile looks phony; sometimes a forced smile looks frozen on your face. When you smile often, your smile will become a natural part of your demeanor.

Make eye contact. This is one of the most important components of communication, yet it can be a tough habit to get into. If you are uncomfortable making eye contact when you speak, first try to get into the habit of making eye contact when you listen. Nod, smile, stay interested. When you are comfortable doing that, make a conscious effort to look at the other person when you speak. When your eyes stray, bring them back. Wandering eyes sends a message that you are bored or more interested in someone or something other than the person you are with. Making eye contact is a powerful tool. Eye contact shows you are interested, honest, and confident.

Maintain good posture. Standing straight also sends the message that you are confident. Get in the habit of holding your head high, but keep it in a relaxed position. When you hold your head comfortably high, your body will naturally have good posture. Try this posture exercise: pretend you have a string attached to the top of your head. Imagine the string is being pulled straight up until you are standing tall and holding your head in a comfortable position. When you find yourself slumping, do the string exercise.

Get enough rest. It is really tough to operate at peak performance when you are tired. When you are tired, you run the risk of being lethargic, making poor decisions, being lax in your appearance, becoming short with people, and being unable to focus and listen. When you are rested you will think clearly, care about the way you look, have a positive attitude, and stay attentive.

Keep your energy level steady. Think about your energy level. Do you have high energy in the morning, but become tired after lunch? Are you numb until you have your morning coffee? Do you have mood swings? Eating sugar in the morning causes some people to crash before lunch. Eating a heavy lunch causes some people to crash in the afternoon. Try changing your diet to healthy and nutritious foods that will give you long-lasting energy. When you start feeling tired at work, try doing a few stretches. These can even be done inconspicuously at your desk or work station. Maintaining good posture also helps keep your energy level up.

HOW COULD THE EMPLOYEE HAVE IMPROVED HIS NONVERBAL COMMUNICATION?

Steve begins to give his order. "I'll have a turkey and Swiss on whole wheat with mayo and tomatoes. . . ." As he speaks he notices that the employee looks directly at him before writing down the item. He smiles often, his posture tells Steve he is interested, and he nods occasionally as Steve speaks.

This time he sent a message to Steve that he was interested in him as a customer.

STEP 3: Putting Words Together: Grammar Usage

Proper grammar is critical to effective communication. When you use proper grammar, it is easier to send the right message. Save the *"Hey man"* and *"Whaddyawant"* for your friends.

Reflect your company's personality. At work you are the voice for your business, and you should always choose words that reflect your company's personality. In a deli setting, the business personality will be fairly casual. In a five-star restaurant, it will be more formal. If you are unclear how you should speak to customers, how friendly or casual you should be, ask your manager for guidance.

Speak clearly. Using overly casual terms or running words together can be difficult for some people to understand. Get in the habit of always sounding out words in their correct form. Say *"Hello"* or *"Hi"* in place of *"Hey man."* Say *"What would you like to order?"* or *"How can I help you?"* in place of *"Whaddyawant?"* Speak clearly, and you will present yourself as an intelligent, competent person.

Use everyday language. In Step 1, you learned that choosing the right words helps you send the right message to your listener. When you have a choice between two words, always opt for the simpler of the two. Keep your words short and simple whenever you can. They are easy for everyone to understand, and you do not risk the chance of sending the wrong message.

Avoid using slang, jargon, company terms, and technical language. Your customers are not likely to know company terms, acronyms, and jargon, so stick to common, generic words. Most customers will not understand the technical terms you use. When you need to give technical explanations convert difficult-to-understand words into words to which your customer will relate. Always speak the language that your customers will understand. Try to match your speech to each customer's level of comprehension.

HOW COULD THE EMPLOYEE HAVE IMPROVED HIS GRAMMAR?

The employee greets Steve by saying, "Hi, Welcome to Max's Deli. How are you doing?"

When it is time to take the order, he responds to Steve's statement about being in a hurry with, "Absolutely. I'll put a rush on it. What can I get you?"

The employee used good grammar and sounded each word out. His words were appropriate for an employee working in a deli.

STEP 4: Asking the Correct Questions and Answering the Questions Correctly

We ask questions for many reasons. As customers, we ask questions to gather new information and acquire additional information. Employees ask questions to figure out how to solve a customer's problem or to resolve a customer's complaint.

There are two types of questions: open and closed. Open questions require more than a yes or no answer and encourage the responder to give information. Closed questions require only a one word or short answer and are often used for clarification.

Keep your questions simple. Stick to one type of question. When you lump the two types of questions together, you run the risk that your customers may not register all the responses. If a question is long and involved, break it down. When you need to ask a series of questions, try interjecting some of the following statements in place of questions, so you will not sound as though you are interrogating your customer with a barrage of questions.

> *"Tell me about. . . ."*
> *"Tell me more."*
> *"I'd like to get more information on. . . ."*
> *"Describe. . . ."*

Ask open questions when you need information. Questions that require more than a one word or short answer will get the customer talking. Open questions begin with *what, why,* and *how.* Use open questions when you need information from a customer. Use open questions when you begin the questioning process to encourage your customer to talk.

> *"How do you. . . ."*
> *"What would you like. . . ."*
> *"What else. . . ."*
> *"What are. . . ."*
> *"Why is that. . . ."*
> *"How are you. . . ."*

"What would happen. . . ."
"How will. . . ."
"What type. . . ."

 Be careful when asking a "why" question. For example, *"Why do you want to do that?"* may put your customer on the defensive. She might reply, *"It's none of your business."* Smiling and using a reflective or helpful tone indicates you are asking out of interest to learn more about your customer's needs.

Ask closed questions to control the conversation. When you need short answers to clarify information or when you need a specific yes, no, or short answer, choose closed questions. Questions beginning with *is, are, do, can,* or *will* require only a yes or no answer. Questions beginning with *who, would, how,* or *where* require a short answer. Closed questions are good to use toward the end of the questioning portion of your contact to narrow down the information you need to help your customer.

"Are you. . . ."
"Do you think. . . ."
"Will you. . . ."
"Would you like. . . ."
"Where do you. . . ."
"How many. . . ."
"Who will. . . ."

Before answering a customer's question, make sure you understand it. If you do not clearly understand the question, recap the question or ask a clarifying question rather than guessing an answer. It is better to ask another question than to answer the wrong question. Also, never answer a question unless you are sure your answer is accurate. It is better to say *"I don't know,"* than to give an answer that may be incorrect. If you do not know, say so; follow up with *"I'll find out for you."*

Try to give more than a one word answer. No matter which questioning technique customers use, try to answer as though the question is open ended. Try to give customers sufficient information to help them make decisions. Giving more than a one word answer can have an added bonus: You can generate sales. For example, if Steve asks, *"Do you have potato salad?"* The employee can answer *"Yes."* Or . . . *"We sure do. We also have coleslaw, baked beans, and pasta salad."* Now Steve has many options from which to choose. He may decide to order, not only the potato salad, but other sides as well, helping to improve the deli's bottom line.

Try to erase the words *I can't* from your vocabulary. Always try to focus on what you can do. If a customer asks you to do something you cannot do, say, *"Here's what I can do for you. . . ."*

When a customer asks for another employee who is not available, never say that the employee is at lunch, on break, went home early, has not come in yet, or that you do not know where the employee is. Rather, say, "_____ *is unavailable now. How can I help you?"* or *"_____ is out of the office now. I'll be happy to help you."*

HOW COULD THE EMPLOYEE IMPROVE HIS QUESTIONING TECHNIQUES?

The customer finishes his order. ". . . a ham on rye with mustard and a pastrami on rye with mustard."

"What else would you like?"

"Do you have potato salad?"

"We sure do. We also have cole slaw, baked beans, and pasta salad."

"I'll take a side order of potato salad."

"Would you like any other sides?"

"No thanks."

"No problem. Just one more thing, do you want spicy or regular mustard on the sandwiches?"

"Regular."

The employee asked an open question to see if Steve wanted anything else. He asked a closed question when he was finishing the order, then followed up with another closed question to clarify the type of mustard.

STEP 5: When the Customer Says No

You will absolutely, definitely, positively, have to handle customers who say no. When you offer a valid solution and your customer says no, your job is to uncover the reasons for your customer's objections. If you work in sales, it may also be your job to find ways to convince the customer to say yes. The bottom line, always, is to do what is right for your customer. Never offer or try to sell a customer something she does not need just to make a sale. When you get to the real reason for the objection, you will figure out the best solution for that particular customer.

Listen to the customer's objection. When a customer says no, an objection is made to your proposed solution. To learn the reason behind the no, ask a combination of open and closed questions. You need to understand why the customer is saying no so you can best help her. For example, you just made a sales proposal for a complete home security system, and the customer says no. You might ask, *"What type of security are you interested in for your home?"* The customer's responses might be: *"Something a little cheaper"* or *"This one seems too complicated for my needs."*

Acknowledge the objection. Always validate the customer's reason, then respond with a positive statement. *"I can understand the price may seem high, but our system offers full security in case of fire and break in. When you consider that, it isn't as expensive as it seems."* Or *"At first it may seem complicated, but once you learn how to use it, it becomes second nature."* Doing this shows you empathize with the customer's objection, while adding another benefit to the solution you proposed.

Follow up with a question. The customer objected. You listened to the customer's objection, acknowledged it, and gave more information about your proposal. Next, you need to follow up. *"How does that sound?"* *"What do you think about that?"* By following up with a clarifying question, you will know how to proceed.

Consider the customer's answer. The customer's response will determine whether she is objecting because she does not agree with your proposal or whether she is looking for more information. If the customer responds with something like, *"How much did you say it will cost?"* she is interested in more information about the product. However, if she answers, *"I really can't afford that,"* proceed with caution. If you have other products to offer, you can ask, *"What were you looking to spend?"* The customer's response will help you determine whether to continue.

Always be truthful when stating your point of view or the benefits of a product. In other words, never try to make a sale or glorify the point you are trying to make to get the customer to agree with you. When you are not truthful, you will come across in a phony manner and the customer will figure out what you are doing.

HOW COULD THE EMPLOYEE HANDLE STEVE'S OBJECTION?

"Would you like any other sides?"

"No thanks."

"Nothing for anyone else?"

"No one mentioned anything. I wouldn't know what to order."

"I understand, but potato salad would be a good choice. We do have a larger size."

"Hmm, I'm not sure."

"The larger size only costs a dollar more than the price for the side order size. How does that sound?"

"Only a dollar more? OK, that sounds good."

"Great. Just one more thing, do you want spicy or regular mustard?"

"Regular."

When Steve said no, the employee gave him another option, then asked a follow-up question. If Steve said no again, it would be time to move on.

STEP 6: Listening Actively

In Step 1, you learned that it is impossible to speak *and* listen at the same time and do both well. Did you ever try to do both at the same time? Not easy, is it? Speaking is important because you are delivering a message, but listening is often more important than speaking. Without the ability to listen well, communication can never be effective. If you do not listen to the message, you might easily give the wrong response.

Focus entirely on your customer. Think of the customer you are helping as the only customer in your business. When you do this, you will be able to give your full attention to that customer. When you are listening to the customer, stay interested, even if your customer's message is long. When that happens, you can show empathy in your facial expressions or by nodding to show you are staying with the customer. When you nod occasionally and say something like, *"I see,"* *"tell me more,"* or *"hmm,"* you show you are still listening. If your customer rambles or gets off track, you may politely interrupt and ask some clarifying questions to take control of the conversation.

 If someone else interrupts you, and it is an avoidable interruption, explain to the interrupter that you will be with him as soon as you are done helping your customer. If it is an unavoidable interruption, excuse yourself momentarily from your customer to answer the other person. Quickly return your attention and apologize for the interruption.

Listen completely. When you try to listen and talk at the same time, you do not do either one effectively. Pay attention to the speaker. You are going to get the ball tossed back to you and, when it is your turn to speak, you will want the other person to pay attention to you. Try not to think of your response when the speaker is still talking. Wait until the message is winding down before thinking how you want to respond. Unless you hear the customer's complete statement or question, you might come up with the incorrect response.

Remain objective; do not judge. Before coming to a conclusion or making a judgment, gather as much information as you can. This will help you avoid jumping to conclusions. If you are not sure you understand correctly, paraphrase the customer's words or ask more questions to gather additional information.

Never assume you know what your customers want. If you are unsure, ask a clarifying question.

Listen for what is not said. You learned about nonverbal communication and how important it is to pay attention to your mannerisms. It is also important to pay attention to your customers' nonverbal signals to see if their words match their emotions. Pay attention to what your customers are really saying. If a customer appears on edge, upset, or angry, show empathy in your replies.

HOW COULD THE EMPLOYEE SHOW HE WAS ACTIVELY LISTENING?

"OK, you mentioned you were in a hurry so I'll put a rush on your order. It should be out very soon."

Throughout their interaction, the employee made eye contact as he wrote down Steve's order. He asked questions to clarify the order. He could tell Steve was in a hurry, so he responded accordingly.

 **PICTURE THIS**

Steve stops at the local deli for lunch. He is in a hurry to place the order for himself and his coworkers and is greeted by an employee who looks at him, smiles, and enthusiastically says, "Hi, Welcome to Max's Deli. How are you doing?"

"I'm doing great, thanks, but I am in a hurry. Is it possible to get my order quickly?"

"Absolutely. I'll put a rush on it. What can I get you?"

Steve begins to give his order, "I'll have a turkey and Swiss on whole wheat with mayo and tomatoes. . . ." As he speaks he notices the employee looks directly at him, before writing down the item. He smiles often, his posture tells Steve he is interested, and he nods occasionally as Steve speaks.

The customer finishes his order, "a ham on rye with mustard and a pastrami on rye with mustard."

"What else would you like?"

"Do you have potato salad?"

"We sure do. We also have cole slaw, baked beans, and pasta salad."

"I'll take a side order of potato salad."

"Would you like any other sides?"

"No thanks."

"Nothing for anyone else?"

"No one mentioned anything. I wouldn't know what to order."

"I understand, but potato salad would be a good choice. We do have a larger size."

"Hmm, I'm not sure."

"The large size only costs a dollar more than the price for the side order size. How does that sound?"

"Only a dollar more? OK, that sounds good."

"Great. Just one more thing, do you want spicy or regular mustard?"

"Regular."

"OK, you mentioned you were in a hurry so I'll put a rush on your order. It should be out very soon."

No matter where you work, you can apply the principles of communicating effectively to your interactions with your customers.

Effective Communication
KEY POINTS

STEP 1: Saying What You Mean and Meaning What You Say

Choose the right words

Make sure your tone fits the message you are sending

Add welcome words to your vocabulary

Keep business conversations professional

STEP 2: What You Don't Say: Nonverbal Communication

Actions speak louder than words

Smile often

Make eye contact

Maintain good posture

Get enough rest

Keep your energy level steady

STEP 3: Putting Words Together: Grammar Usage

Reflect your company's personality

Speak clearly

Use everyday language

Avoid using slang, jargon, company terms, and technical language

STEP 4: Asking the Correct Questions and Answering the Questions Correctly

Keep your questions simple

Ask open questions when you need information

Ask closed questions to control the conversation

Before answering a customer's question, make sure you understand it

Try to give more than a one word answer

STEP 5: When the Customer Says No

Listen to the customer's objection

Acknowledge the objection

Follow up with a question

Consider the customer's answer

STEP 6: Listening Actively

Focus entirely on your customer

Listen completely

Remain objective; do not judge

Listen for what is not said

Effective Communication
PRACTICE LESSON

STEP 1: Saying What You Mean and Meaning What You Say

Make a list of words and phrases you will incorporate into your vocabulary.

_____

_____

_____

_____

STEP 2: What You Don't Say: Nonverbal Communication

Write examples of what you will do to improve your nonverbal communication.

_____

_____

_____

_____

STEP 3: Putting Words Together: Grammar Usage

Think about your grammar and list some things you can do to improve it.

_____

_____

_____

_____

STEP 4: Asking the Correct Questions and Answering the Questions Correctly

Think about your typical customer contacts and write examples of open and closed questions you will use.

_____

_____

_____

_____

STEP 5: When the Customer Says No

Think about a recent customer contact in which the customer objected. Using the questioning techniques, write how you would handle the customer.

_____

_____

_____

_____

STEP 6: Listening Actively

Write examples of how you plan to improve your listening skills.

_____

_____

_____

_____

Think About . . .

Have **you** ever assumed you know what your customers want?

Cindy and her husband, Jerry, met their friends for dinner at a restaurant they were trying for the first time. They had not seen each other in a while and looked forward to an enjoyable and relaxed evening.

As soon as they were seated, the server came to take drink orders. He was pleasant and quickly brought their drinks and bread. He explained the specials and gave them a few minutes to decide.

When he came back, Cindy ordered. "I'd like the salmon, please."

"Good choice," the server replied.

When the entrées came, Cindy was listening to her friend tell a story and did not look at her plate until the server left. Cindy looked at her salmon. Confused, she took a bite. Rather than having a mustard glaze, it was covered in tomatoes and vegetables, which was not appealing to her.

Discreetly, she looked around for the server. He was nowhere to be found.

"What's the matter?" Jerry asked, when he saw she was not eating her salmon.

"This isn't what I ordered. I'd eat it, but I don't care for the way it tastes."

Jerry looked for the server. "It's all right," Cindy said, "don't worry about it." She did not want to detract from their fun evening. She picked at the vegetables as she waited for the server to come back.

Jerry and their friends were almost through with their entrées when the server strolled over to the table. "How is everything?" He asked with an air of confidence.

"This isn't what I ordered. It's supposed to have a mustard glaze."

"This is one of the specials. I thought that's what you wanted."

"No, I wanted the salmon on the regular menu."

"Oh. How about if I give you a free dessert to make up for that?" Not waiting for a reply, he walked away.

Cindy was upset. Jerry and their friends were appalled.

"I can't believe he didn't offer to bring you what you wanted."

"Free dessert? He should have done something more to make up for that."

"He shouldn't charge you for something you didn't order."

When the server came back, he cleared the plates, looked at Cindy's salmon, and said with a chuckle, "I'm sure you don't want that wrapped. What would you like for dessert?"

What was a fun evening now turned to a discussion about the server's attitude. Cindy could not believe he assumed he knew what she wanted.

Normally they were generous tippers. Not this evening. Not only did the waiter assume he knew what Cindy wanted, he made little effort to make things right.

Leaving the restaurant, they said, "With that kind of service, we won't be back here anytime soon."

ASSUMING WHAT SOMEONE WANTS CAN BE EXPENSIVE.
IT CAN COST YOU YOUR CUSTOMERS.

Effective Communication
QUICK QUOTES

Actions speak louder than words

Try very hard to avoid saying no

Erase the words *I can't* from your vocabulary

Tell customers what you *can* do

Never use inappropriate language with a customer

Listen, listen, listen

Listen for what is not said

Never jump to conclusions

Use language your customers understand

Display empathy to show your customers you understand

CHAPTER 3

Jumping in with Both Feet: Relationship Building

TO PROVIDE THE BEST POSSIBLE SERVICE, YOU MUST GET CLOSE TO YOUR CUSTOMERS BY BUILDING A STRONG RELATIONSHIP WITH THEM.

Did you know that every customer contact results in a relationship? You may not realize it, but even when customers only do business with a company once, they remember and judge the company by their relationship with the employees. Whether their relationship is good or bad, they will remember. They are also likely to tell others. People talk. They share their experiences with others.

What Are People Saying About You?

Relationship building is the cornerstone of customer service. Remember, to your customers you are the company. Customers judge a business by their interactions with its employees. From the moment a customer forms his first impression to the moment you complete your interaction with him, you have a valuable opportunity to build a strong relationship. The same applies to those customers who may not come back. When you interact positively and go out of your way to help each customer, you build a relationship. Those customers will remember the great service and will tell others about their experiences.

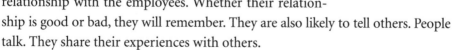

When you are courteous and have a positive attitude toward your customers, you show that you care. When you demonstrate good communication skills by thinking before you speak, keeping your nonverbal body language relaxed and open, and using correct grammar, you present yourself as intelligent and confident. When you ask the correct questions to help the customer and answer all questions the customer asks you, you present yourself as a competent employee. When listening carefully, you demonstrate that you are truly interested in each and every customer.

So far you are off to a good start. The next step is learning how to build relationships. Customers, whether they do business with you repeatedly or only one time, are all equally important. Every customer deserves the same level of service.

You interact with customers in two ways. You work to build new relationships, and you work to maintain ongoing relationships. Both types of interactions are equally important. Without new business relationships, your company will not grow. Without ongoing business relationships, you will not develop a loyal customer base. The principles of basic courtesies and effective communication result in building and maintaining positive relationships.

Your relationship begins when a customer forms a first impression of you and your company. It continues when you establish a rapport. Think, for a moment, about a personal relationship you are or were in. When you first met that special person, you probably made small talk to see if you had something in common. When you discovered that you shared common ground, you made the decision to take your relationship to the next level by going on a date.

The purpose of business relationships, of course, is not to result in dates, but during those first few minutes with a customer it is equally important to find common ground to begin building a relationship. Establishing a rapport with your customer is the first step to finding something in common. You may do this by asking a question as simple as, *"How are you today?,"* and then listening to the customer's response: *"Fine, thanks,"* or *"I'm not doing well at all."*

From these first few words with a customer, you have the opportunity to respond in a positive and upbeat manner. To the customer who is not doing well at all, you may say, *"I'm sorry to hear that. How can I help you?"* Showing interest and doing what you can to take care of the customer's request will make the customer feel valued.

When customers do repeat business, you have the opportunity to maintain an on-going relationship by remembering them, by remembering something about them, and by learning their tastes and preferences. And for the customer who was not having a good day before, you might say, *"Hi Mrs. Adams, I hope you're having a better day today."* Think how special Mrs. Adams will feel knowing that she was important enough to you to remember something about her.

You will deal with many different types of customers. Learning how to interact positively with various personality types will enable you to handle any type of customer in any type of situation. You will be on your way to knowing how to establish and maintain long-term, high-quality relationships with all your customers.

PICTURE THIS

Sarah is an unlikely customer service employee. She is home from college for summer break and takes a part-time job at a women's clothing shop in the local mall. Sarah has not worked in retail before, and she is unsure about how to interact with customers. Her new job is to greet customers and help them find what they need. On her first day, her manager explains her job duties, shows her where to locate stock in the backroom, and tells her to be friendly to customers.

"Be sure you say hi to the customers when they come in," her manager says as she walks away.

Sarah busies herself folding tops on the front display table.

Beth Adams, meanwhile, is outside the store looking at the clothing display in the window. She comes into the store and notices Sarah.

This is Sarah's first customer. She nervously says, "Hi." She barely speaks above a whisper as she quickly glances at the woman and then back down to her work. Sarah continues to fold the tops while the woman browses.

"Excuse me, can you see if you have this skirt in a size twelve?" Beth asks.

Sarah nods, takes the item from Beth and retreats into the stock room without saying a word or making eye contact. When Sarah comes back she says, "Sorry, we don't have it." She speaks softly and looks at the floor as she speaks.

"Oh, all right. Well, thanks for checking." Beth walks out of the store.

What Went Wrong?

Even though Sarah knew she would have to deal with customers, she did not understand the importance of building customer relationships. She wanted to work in this clothing store to get the employee discount. She never gave much thought to the job duties or the customers.

Her manager showed Sarah where to locate stock in the backroom, showed her how to keep the displays neat, and told her to be friendly to the customers. But, what exactly does *being friendly* mean? To the manager, it might mean something quite different than what Sarah thinks. Unless Sarah knows specifically how she is supposed to interact with customers, she most likely will assume she is being friendly.

How Did the Customer Feel?

How do you think Sarah made the customer feel from the time she came into the store until the time she left?

_____

_____

_____

_____

How do you think Sarah's customer judged her relationship with the store?

_____

_____

_____

_____

We need to back up a moment before we continue. Remember that relationships begin when you establish a rapport with your customers. But to know how to establish a rapport, you need to define three things: Who your customers are; what they expect from your business; and how your company's products and services enhance their lives. When you understand these three things, you will understand your customers' general needs and wants. As a result, you will have a better idea of how to establish a rapport, how to find common ground and relate to your customers, and how to build strong relationships.

Sarah's motivation for working in this store was to get the employee discount. She never thought about the customers she would be helping. She did not understand who her customers were. Were they one-time shoppers or did the store get a lot of repeat business? How did they expect to be treated when they came in? If the store was an expensive designer boutique, the customers would have different expectations than a store that mass markets inexpensive items.

Sarah did not understand what the customers expected from her or the store. How involved was she supposed to be with customers? Was she supposed to help them select outfits? Or did customers come in to browse and want to be left alone? Would she be dealing with the same customers regularly? If so, it would be important for Sarah to introduce herself and get to know her customers and their individual tastes and styles.

Sarah never thought about how the store's products would enhance its customers' lives. Knowing this would enable Sarah to help her customers. If this was an expensive boutique where the customers were interested in labels, Sarah could show customers where to find certain designer items. If the store stocked trendy items, Sarah could show customers the newest items and the hot sellers.

Even in a clothing store where customers may only visit randomly, employees can work on developing relationships with them. Unless Sarah learns some things about her customers, she is going to have a difficult time helping them. Every customer interaction, even short-term ones like Sarah's, results in a relationship. Customers judge a business through their relationships.

Who are your customers?

_____

_____

_____

_____

What do they expect from your company?

_____

_____

_____

_____

How do your company's products and services enhance their lives?

_____

_____

_____

_____

How could knowing these three things have helped Sarah give Beth better service? _____

_____

_____

_____

Most likely Beth did not leave the store with a warm and fuzzy feeling. Sarah did nothing to make Beth want to hurry back. Sarah was unsure how she was supposed to act around customers, but anyone, even someone who is as inexperienced as Sarah, can learn to build positive relationships with customers.

By learning the six steps below you will learn how to build and maintain positive and strong relationships with all your customers.

> **STEP 1: Establishing Rapport**
> **STEP 2: Interacting Positively with Customers**
> **STEP 3: Identifying Customers' Needs**
> **STEP 4: Making the Customer Feel Valued**
> **STEP 5: Maintaining Ongoing Relationships**
> **STEP 6: Different Strokes: Handling Different Types of Customers**

In Sarah's contact with Beth, she could have done many things differently. Sarah also could have asked her manager what she meant when she said to *"be friendly."*

In answer to the questions, you may have written:

How do you think Sarah made the customer feel, from the time she came into the store until the time she left?

Sarah did not make a good first impression. She should have made eye contact with the customer. She should have smiled and greeted the customer to show she was interested in her. When the customer asked for help, she should have said, "I'll be happy to check on that," or "Absolutely. I'll be glad to see if we have that."

How do you think Sarah's customer judged her relationship with the store?

The customer felt Sarah and the store management did not care about her. She did not seem very satisfied when she left the store.

Finally, think about this. How could Sarah be sure that she understood her relationship to the customers? She could have asked her manager questions during her training. For example, when the manager said to be friendly, Sarah could have asked, *"Am I supposed to ask all the customers if they need help?"* This would also show her manager that she was interested in doing a good job.

STEP 1: Establishing Rapport

Establishing a rapport begins the moment you start communicating with your customers. Smiling at a customer can help establish a rapport by showing you are interested. How you establish a rapport depends on your customer interactions. Think about how you answered these questions: Who are your customers; what do they expect from your company; and how do your company's products and services enhance their lives?

Who are your customers? Are they men, women, tweens, teens, young adults, or all age groups?

What do they expect from your company? Quality products? Good value? The best prices? Quick service? Products that will enhance their self-image? A large selection? The latest styles?

How do your company's products and services enhance the customers' lives? Do they make the customers' lives easier? Are they a necessity? Do they make your customers feel good about themselves?

When you know the answers to these questions, you will have a good idea about how to relate to your customers. Armed with this knowledge, you can begin to establish a rapport with your customers. Establishing a rapport is the first step of relationship building. You begin every relationship by laying building blocks on top of the basic foundation you learned in Chapter 1.

Be friendly. No matter who your customers are, everyone appreciates someone who is friendly. When you smile and offer a friendly greeting, you put your customers at ease. You show them, from the start, that you are a person who is approachable and willing to help.

Be interested. The smile and greeting also show that you are interested. When you ask people how they are doing or ask how you can help, you are conveying the message that you are interested. Being interested means listening when customers respond. Imagine how you would sound if you asked a customer how he was doing, he said, *"I'm having the worst day of my life. Really awful,"* and with no emotion you responded, *"Oh."* Not very interested, right? The customer most likely would be wondering why you bothered to ask. Being interested means listening and responding accordingly. Being interested means thinking of ways to brighten other people's days.

Be sensitive. When the customer said he was having the worst day of his life you could have said, *"Oh my gosh. I'm sorry to hear that. What can I do to make your day better?"* Not only are you interested, you are sensitive to the customer's situation. Being sensitive means being empathetic and considerate of other people's situations. Even if you can not personally understand or relate to what the customer is saying, you can be sensitive in your response.

Be trustful. The best way to demonstrate that you can be trusted is by being honest and ethical in everything you do. When you always act with integrity, your personality reflects your honesty. If you are friendly and helpful with a customer and later make fun of him within earshot of other customers, you do not come across as being a trustful person. Being trustful includes treating people with dignity and respect.

Find common ground. When you listen to your customer's statements and responses, try to find something you have in common. To the customer who is having a bad day, you might respond, *"I'm sorry to hear that. I had one of those days yesterday. Nothing seemed to go right for me."* The customer will appreciate that you can relate to having a bad day. Even if you did not have a bad day to relate to, there are other ways to find common ground. Empathize with the customer. Ask a question. Show interest. In other situations, you can relate by complimenting the customer on something she is wearing, by saying something about yourself, or even by talking about the weather.

HOW COULD SARAH HAVE ESTABLISHED RAPPORT WITH HER CUSTOMER?

"Be sure you say hi to the customers when they come in," her manager says as she walks away.

"I have a question," Sarah stops her. "When I say hi to customers, am I supposed to ask if they need help or should I leave them alone?"

"That's a good question. Most of our customers come in to browse so we usually leave them alone. But I do want you to let them know you are here to help if they need anything. When a customer comes in, smile, look at her, and say something like, 'Hi, how are you today? If you need anything, I'll be happy to help you find it.' That way the customer knows we're going to leave her alone to browse, but will be available to help."

"OK." Sarah busies herself folding tops on the front display table.

Beth Adams, meanwhile, is outside the store looking at the clothing display in the window. She comes into the store and notices Sarah.

This is Sarah's first customer. She is nervous, but knows what she needs to do. She looks at Beth, smiles, and says, "Hi, how are you doing today?"

Beth smiles back. "I'm fine, thanks, how are you?"

"It's my first day so I don't know yet. I'm a little nervous."

"I know how that feels. I'm sure you'll do just fine."

"If you need anything, I'll be happy to help you find it."

"Thanks, I'm looking for a skirt. I'll look around."

"OK. We have skirts in great summer colors."

Beth smiles and walks away.

Even though Sarah felt awkward, she knew what she needed to do. She showed she was friendly by smiling and greeting Beth. She demonstrated she was interested in Beth by listening and commenting on the skirts in great summer colors. When she told Beth it was her first day and she was nervous, Beth could relate to her feelings and they found common ground. Sarah established a rapport with Beth.

STEP 2: Interacting Positively with Customers

Once you establish a rapport, continue building your relationships by interacting with your customers in a positive manner. When you are positive and upbeat, people will respond likewise. It is hard to stay down with someone who is upbeat. What type of people do you like to be around? Those who bring you up? Or those who drag you down? At work, be a person who brings others up.

Be helpful. Show your customers you care. Go the extra mile for them. Do something to make other people feel good about themselves. Set a personal goal to help someone every day. You will feel better when you meet that goal. It is a great personal habit to get into.

Be committed. When you commit yourself to your company and to your customers, you will look for ways to make things better. No matter what you do today, do your best. Give today and every day 110%. Give your customers 110%.

Be a problem solver. Be part of the solution rather than part of the problem. Look for answers rather than focusing on what is wrong. When you adopt a problem-solving approach you will find it hard to be negative. People who focus on problems complain; people who focus on solutions find ways to make a difference.

Be credible. This means being knowledgeable about your products and your company. Customers appreciate nice employees, but they value knowledgeable employees. Learn as much as you can about your product line. If you need additional technical training, ask your manager for it.

Believe in your products. No matter what your company manufactures or sells, whether it is life insurance or clothing, you need to believe in your products. Otherwise you will never come across sincerely. Sincerity is borne out of believing in what you do. Believing that your products will help your customers is crucial to doing the right thing for them. It does not matter what line of work you are in, when you truly believe that your company's products can help your customers, you will promote your products, your company, and yourself in a positive and sincere manner.

HOW COULD SARAH HAVE INTERACTED POSITIVELY WITH BETH?

Sarah continues to fold the tops while Beth browses.

"Excuse me, can you see if you have this skirt in a size twelve?" Beth asks.

Sarah takes the skirt from Beth and says, "Yes, I'll be happy to. This is a great skirt, and I love this shade of green."

"I love it too. I hope you have it, I could use a green skirt."

"I'll be right back."

Sarah hurries into the stock room. She comes back with a different style green skirt and says, "I'm sorry, we don't have that skirt in your size. I don't know if you saw this one. I brought it because you mentioned you wanted a green skirt."

"Thanks, but that isn't exactly what I was looking for."

Sarah was helpful. She demonstrated she was solution oriented by bringing a different green skirt. She showed she believed in her products by saying that Beth made a great choice.

STEP 3: Identifying Customers' Needs

Customers come into your business for a reason. Sometimes they are not very clear about their needs. Beth was specific when she mentioned she needed a green skirt. This helped Sarah come up with an alternative option. If Beth had not mentioned a green skirt, Sarah would not have known her needs. While this is a simplistic example, the principle is the same, whether you sell clothing or computer systems. When you deal with customers, your job is to uncover their needs.

Ask questions. In Chapter 2 you learned about open and closed questions. When customers do not know how to tell you what they need, it is your job to figure out what they need. Sometimes customers are not even sure they know what they need. Use open questions to get the customer talking. Remember, questions that begin with *what, why,* and *how* encourage customers to talk. Use closed questions to clarify an answer. Closed questions begin with *who, would, how,* and *where*. A question beginning with *how* can be either open or closed: Open, *How do you think you would use this?* Closed, *How many times a week will you use it?*

Summarize customers' needs. After you have asked enough questions to determine your customer's needs, summarize your understanding of what the customer has told you. For example, *"From what I understand, your son has allergies, and you are looking for a vacuum cleaner that will remove the greatest number allergens and is the least costly"* or *"You mentioned that you got your bill, and you were overcharged for. . . ."* If your understanding is incorrect, ask more open and closed questions until you get it right.

Recommend appropriate solutions. When you ask enough questions, you get enough information to recommend the best solution. If your job is to sell products, you can make an appropriate proposal. If you handle billing issues and miscellaneous problems, you can find a workable solution. Make sure that your recommendations are based on what the customer told you. Refer to things the customer said when making your recommendation. *"This is our most economic vacuum, and it will remove 99% of all allergens. With your son's allergies, you want to make sure your vacuum picks up as many of allergen particles as possible."*

Handle objections. Follow the steps you learned in Chapter 2. Listen to the customer's objection. Acknowledge it. Follow up with a question. Consider the customer's answer. Following up on the vacuum cleaner sale, the customer says *"Thanks, I'll think about it."* You respond, *"What questions do you have about this one?"* *"None, but it's more than I wanted to spend."* *"I can understand that, but this product is the most efficient for removing allergens. We do have cheaper models that I can show you, but none of them work as well as this one."* Answer the customer's silent question, *What is this going to do for me?* When you can answer this question, you will be better able to get past the customer's objections.

HOW COULD SARAH HAVE USED QUESTIONING TECHNIQUES TO UNCOVER BETH'S NEEDS?

"Thanks, but that isn't exactly what I was looking for."

"What type of skirt are you interested in?"

"I prefer longer skirts."

"What other colors would you be interested in?"

"I really could use green. I suppose I could use a khaki one, too."

"Do you like prints?"

"No, I only wear solids."

"OK, a longer skirt in a solid green or khaki. Why don't I check in the back to see if we have any?"

"Would you? That would be great."

Sarah asked the customer questions to determine exactly what she was looking for, then she recapped what the customer said to make sure she understood. Once she was clear, she made a recommendation to look for another style of skirt.

STEP 4: Making the Customer Feel Valued

When you establish a rapport, interact positively, identify customer needs to make a valid recommendation, and make customers feel valued, you are on your way to building strong relationships. Whether your interaction is a one-time conversation or an ongoing interaction with a customer who does repeat business with your company, your primary job is to communicate effectively and build positive relationships.

Go out of your way for your customers. Do what you can to help them. Try to give them more than they asked for. When a customer asks a question, give a thorough explanation rather than a one word answer. Your customers will know when you go out of your way for them. Sarah could have easily let Beth walk out the door when she could not find the skirt she wanted. By going out of her way, she not only made Beth feel valued, she also had the possibility of making a sale.

Validate customers' decisions. Even if you do not agree with customers' choices, always validate their decisions. If the vacuum salesperson was not able to make the sale, he could validate the customer's decision by saying, *"I understand how you feel. This brand is costly."* How would Beth feel if Sarah said, *"You want green? Green is such a drab color. Why not go for a bright color like pink?"* Sarah validated Beth's decision to buy a green skirt by saying that was a great color. When she could not find that particular skirt in green she asked Beth what she was interested in. This also validated Beth's feelings.

Instill positive feelings. Never make customers feel bad about their decisions. Think how the mother would feel if the salesperson said, *"I guess your son will have to deal with the allergens in your house."* Rather, he could say, *"It's a big decision. I'll be happy to help you if you have any more questions about it."*

HOW COULD SARAH MAKE BETH FEEL VALUED?

Sarah returns with a skirt. "I found this khaki skirt. How do you like it?"

After looking it over, Beth says, "Thanks for looking, but I still like the style of the green one better."

"I understand and I appreciate that you really liked that skirt. I'm sorry I couldn't help you find something."

Sarah went out of her way to find another skirt, but when Beth said it was not what she was looking for, Sarah validated Beth's decision by saying she understood. She instilled positive feelings by assuring Beth that she appreciated her decision. She had no other styles to show Beth so that was as far as she went.

STEP 5: Maintaining Ongoing Relationships

Once you build strong relationships with customers, your work is not done. In any relationship, whether business or personal, you have to work to maintain the relationship. Customers come back a second time because you established a relationship with them. Imagine how valued they will feel if you remember them? Because Sarah went out of her way to help Beth, Beth is likely to return. That is the way to build customer loyalty. But, if Beth goes back and Sarah does not remember her, Beth will not be as likely to maintain a business relationship.

Remember your customers. Nothing makes a customer feel more valued than being remembered. Remember your repeat customers and acknowledge them. Customers who do repeat business with a company appreciate being recognized. When customers are treated as though they are invisible, they might just become invisible.

Learn customers' names. When customers come into your business repeatedly, make it a point to learn their names. People love hearing their names, especially when they come into a business. Addressing a customer by name will let her know she is important to you. If you do not know the customer well, use the last name. *"Hi Mrs. Adams, how are you today?"* Leave it up to Mrs. Adams to tell you whether you should call her by her first name.

Remember something about your customers. Remember the customer who was having the worst day? Think how he would feel if next time you said, *"Hi, how are you doing today? I hope you're having a better day than the last time you were in."* Everyone appreciates an employee with a good memory. This shows your customers that you value your relationship with them.

Learn your customers' preferences. If you deal with the same customers repeatedly, get to know what they like. If you have too many customers to remember each one's tastes, you could start a card file or a computer file and note your repeat customers' preferences and other information you might want to remember about them. Next time they come in, try to incorporate their preferences into your conversation. Your customers will be impressed that you remembered.

Try to do something special every now and then for your repeat customers. It can be something as simple as taking the time to talk to them and showing new products that might interest them or asking if they would like a cup of coffee. Show your repeat customers that you appreciate them.

HOW COULD SARAH MAINTAIN AN ONGOING RELATIONSHIP WITH HER CUSTOMERS?

The following week, Sarah spots Beth in the store. She walks over to her. "Hi. You know I thought of you the other day."

"You did?"

"I sure did. We got some new green skirts in, and I was hoping I'd see you. We still have some in stock. Would you like me to show them to you?"

"Yes! I can't believe you remembered."

Not only did Sarah remember Beth, she remembered that Beth was looking for a green skirt. Next time Beth needs clothes, where do you think she will go? Sarah built a relationship with Beth and now she is working to maintain it.

STEP 6: Different Strokes: Handling Different Types of Customers

Most of your customers will be average people with average needs. Most of your customers will be pleasant people who appreciate your help. Some customers, though, will test your skills and, at times, your patience.

Besides the average, everyday people with whom you regularly interact, here are some other customer "types" and tips on how to interact positively with them.

The pushy, obnoxious customer—remain calm. Maintain a professional demeanor. Smile. Try to put the customer at ease. Speak softly and control your voice inflection. Never take on the same tone this type of customer uses with you. Speak in a positive, upbeat tone of voice. When you stay calm, you stay in control. When you stay in control, you will be able to help this type of customer without coming unglued. Remember, pushy, obnoxious customers are not like this only with you. This is part of their personalities and perhaps being pushy is the only way they know how to act. In other words, do not take their behavior personally.

The timid, indecisive customer—be patient. Help draw these customers out and get them to talk more. Ask open ended questions. Listen closely to their responses and try to guide them to give you enough information to help them reach a decision. Some people have a difficult time reaching any decision. Some people are naturally shy. Be sensitive to timid, indecisive customers and help them become more talkative by asking questions and encouraging them to talk.

The overly friendly, flirty customer—be professional. Keep your end of the conversation on business. These customers can be difficult to handle because they do not see their behavior as being out of line. It is up to you to control the conversation. Do not foster overly friendly or flirty behavior by being overly friendly in return. Guide your conversation back to business. If a flirty customer continues, give a gentle reminder that you want to help—with a business solution.

The culturally different customer—be tolerant. We live in a society made up of many cultures, languages, and customs, yet, people often do not know how to talk or act in the presence of a person from another culture. Kindness, a smile, honesty, and empathy translate into any language and across any barrier. People who do not look like us or act like we do can make us uncomfortable. By learning to be tolerant of differences, you will overcome any cultural obstacles.

A special note on people with disabilities—be respectful. People with disabilities want to be treated like everyone else. Make eye contact and speak in your normal tone and pace of speech. Once you get used to dealing with people with disabilities, you will see that they want to be treated like anyone else, with dignity and respect.

When interacting with people with disabilities, focus on the person first and the disability second. Putting the disability first, such as saying "*the handicapped person*", places the focus on the disability rather than on the person. When referring to a person with a disability, use terms such as "*the man who uses a wheelchair*", "*the woman who is blind*", or "*the person with epilepsy*". Terms such as *crippled, retarded, deformed, lame,* or *crazy* are considered unacceptable, so drop these and other terms with negative connotations from your vocabulary. If you do not know how to refer to a person, use the term "person with a disability".

Other tips for interacting with people with disabilities:

→ Offer to shake hands if this is normally how you greet people. It is acceptable to shake a person's left hand. If, after offering your hand, you find the person is unable to shake hands, complete the handshake by placing your hand on the person's right hand.

→ Always ask first if a person wants help.

→ If you don't know what to do to help a person, ask what you should do.

For People Who Use Wheelchairs:

→ Try to place yourself at the person's eye level.

→ Never lean on a wheelchair or hover over the person.

→ Make eye contact and speak directly to the person, not to the person's companion.

For People with Developmental or Cognitive Disabilities:

➜ Speak clearly and use short, easy to understand words.

➜ If the person has difficulty writing, offer to help complete paperwork.

➜ Give the person ample time to formulate thoughts and respond to you.

➜ Refrain from finishing the person's sentence.

For People with Visual Impairments:

➜ Never touch a service dog without first asking permission.

➜ Tell the person about any obstacles in his or her path. "*There are boxes in the aisle ahead, so we'll walk on the left side.*"

➜ When asking the person to take a seat, help him or her touch the chair first.

➜ Verbalize what you are doing to help the person. "*I'm inputting the information into my computer so I can give you an installation date.*"

For People with Hearing Impairments:

➜ Look at the person and speak and enunciate clearly.

➜ Use simple words and short sentences.

For People with Speech Impairments:

➜ Ask the person to repeat if you do not understand, then repeat his/her words back to be sure you understood correctly.

➜ Use closed questions that require short answers.

In all cases, when interacting with people with disabilities, be patient. Also, don't be embarrassed or overly apologetic if you make a blunder.

When you learn to interact with different types of people and personalities, you will confidently handle any customer in any situation. By building and maintaining positive relationships, you are on your way to providing great customer service.

PICTURE THIS

Beth Adams comes into the store and notices Sarah.

This is Sarah's first customer. She is nervous but knows what she needs to do. She looks at Beth, smiles, and says, "Hi, how are you doing today?"

Beth smiles back. "I'm fine, thanks, how are you?"

"It's my first day so I don't know yet. I'm a little nervous."

"I know how that feels. I'm sure you'll do just fine."

"If you need anything, I'll be happy to help you find it."

"Thanks, I'm looking for a skirt. I'll look around."

"OK. We have skirts in great summer colors."

Beth smiles and walks away.

Sarah continues to fold the tops while Beth browses.

"Excuse me, can you see if you have this skirt in a size twelve?" Beth asks.

Sarah takes the skirt from Beth and says, "Yes, I'll be happy to. This is a great skirt and I love this shade of green."

"I love it too. I hope you have it, I could use a green skirt."

"I'll be right back."

Sarah hurries into the stock room. She comes back with a different style green skirt and says, "I'm sorry, we don't have that skirt in your size. I don't know if you saw this one. I brought it because you mentioned you wanted a green skirt."

"Thanks, but that isn't exactly what I was looking for."

"What type of skirt are you interested in?"

"I prefer longer skirts."

"What other colors would you be interested in?"

"I really could use green. I suppose I could use a khaki one, too."

"Do you like prints?"

"No, I only wear solids."

"OK, a longer skirt in a solid green or khaki. Why don't I check in the back to see if we have any?"

"Would you? That would be great."

Sarah returns with a skirt. "I found this khaki skirt. How do you like it?"

After looking it over, Beth says, "Thanks for looking, but I still like the style of the green one better."

"I understand and I appreciate that you really liked that skirt. I'm sorry I couldn't help you find something."

The following week, Sarah spots Beth in the store. She walks over to her. "Hi. You know I thought of you the other day."

"You did?"

"I sure did. We got some new green skirts in, and I was hoping I'd see you. We still have some in stock. Would you like me to show them to you?"

"Yes! I can't believe you remembered."

All your customer interactions may not be this simple or straightforward. Even if your customer contacts are much more involved, practice these steps and you will be able to build and maintain positive relationships with all your customers.

Relationship Building
KEY POINTS

STEP 1: Establishing Rapport

Be friendly

Be interested

Be sensitive

Be trustful

Find common ground

STEP 2: Interacting Positively with Customers

Be helpful

Be committed

Be a problem solver

Be credible

Believe in your products

STEP 3: Identifying Customers' Needs

Ask questions

Summarize customers' needs

Recommend appropriate solutions

Handle objections

STEP 4: Making the Customer Feel Valued

Go out of your way for your customers

Validate customers' decisions

Instill positive feelings

STEP 5: Maintaining Ongoing Relationships

Remember your customers

Learn customers' names

Remember something about your customers

Learn your customers' preferences

STEP 6: Different Strokes: Handling Different Types of Customers

Pushy, obnoxious customers—remain calm

Timid, indecisive customers—be patient

Overly friendly, flirty customers—be professional

Culturally different customers—be tolerant

People with disabilities—be respectful

Relationship Building
PRACTICE LESSON

STEP 1: Establishing Rapport

Think of a typical customer you have. Write down how you can establish a rapport.

_____

_____

_____

_____

STEP 2: Interacting Positively with Customers

What are some ways in which you can interact positively with your typical customer?

_____

_____

_____

_____

STEP 3: Identifying Customers' Needs

What questions can you ask to uncover your customers' needs?

_____

_____

_____

_____

STEP 4: Making the Customer Feel Valued

What are some things you can do to make your customers feel valued?

_____

_____

_____

_____

STEP 5: Maintaining Ongoing Relationships

What are some things you can do to make your repeat customers feel special?

_____

_____

_____

_____

STEP 6: Different Strokes: Handling Different Types of Customers

How will you handle customers who are:

Pushy and obnoxious

_____

_____

_____

_____

Timid or indecisive

_____

_____

_____

_____

Overly friendly and flirty

_____

_____

_____

_____

Culturally different

_____

_____

_____

_____

Disabled

_____

_____

_____

_____

Think About . . .

Have **you** ever blown a relationship because you did not work to maintain it?

Every day Kevin went out to lunch.

Every day he went to the same restaurant.

He sat at the same table and was waited on by the same waitress.

Every day the waitress asked him the same question.

"Hi, what can I get you today?"

Every day he gave the same reply.

"I'll have the special."

One day, his friend invited him to lunch at a new restaurant in town. Kevin went. When they walked into the restaurant, the manager greeted them. "Hi, welcome to the Downtown Diner. Have a seat anywhere you'd like."

They sat, and a waitress came to their table. "Hi guys, how are you doing?" She was cheerful and made them feel comfortable. "What can I get you today?"

"I'll have the special," Kevin said.

"I had that for my lunch, and it's great," she smiled.

Kevin enjoyed his lunch so much he decided to go back the following day. On his third day back, the waitress said, "Hi, it's nice to see you again. The special, right?"

Kevin laughed and nodded. "Hey, ordering the special takes the guesswork out of things. One less decision to make is a good thing."

Kevin was impressed that she not only remembered him, she remembered what he ordered. He thought about the other restaurant. *I went there every day, and they acted like they didn't know me. I've been here three times, and the waitress not only remembers me, she remembers what I order.*

That diner had a new regular. Because this waitress cared enough about Kevin to remember his preference, she made him feel valued as a customer. To Kevin, that was important.

Relationship Building
QUICK QUOTES

Do everything you can to help your customers

Relationships are built on trust

If in doubt, rule in favor of the customer

Find ways to give customers more than they expect

Tell your customers you appreciate their business

When you make a mistake, make it right with the customer

Perception is everything—to your customers; their perception is reality

Try to see things from the customer's perspective

Treat all customers equally

The customer is the reason you have a job

PART II

Putting Your Customers First

CHAPTER 4

Seeing Eye to Eye: Face-to-Face Contacts

CUSTOMERS MAY COME INTO A BUSINESS BECAUSE OF THE PRODUCTS BUT THEY WILL DECIDE TO COME AGAIN BECAUSE OF THE WAY THEY ARE TREATED.

Write down a typical customer contact that is reflective of your face-to-face interactions:

_____

_____

_____

_____

_____

_____

_____

_____

Think about this scenario as you work through this chapter. Use it as the example when answering the practice lesson questions.

Giving exceptional customer service when dealing with customers in person seems pretty simple on *face* value. Why, then, do so many of our interactions with customer service employees leave us feeling empty, or worse yet, invisible?

Customers have been conditioned not to expect much. When you treat customers as though they are important guests you invited into your business, they will feel valued. When you treat customers as though they matter to you, they will feel appreciated.

You already learned that creating a positive first impression will help you build the foundation for providing great customer service. Customers are going to judge you by your initial look, manner, and actions. Did you know that customers also get a first impression of your overall business when they come in? In addition to forming a first impression of you, your customers also judge your company by its look, image, and overall atmosphere.

Put your customer hat back on. Think about some businesses you went into recently. What was your first impression of them? Did you notice that some of them seemed to invite you inside with their warmth, while others felt so chilly you could not wait to leave?

Customers judge a business in its entirety. Their assessment, particularly when forming that crucial first impression, includes how you look and act, how your business looks and feels, and how well you interact with them. Customers may come to your business because of a product or service, but they will decide to stay or leave based on an overall feeling of warmth or coolness. The difference between the two can bring them back or keep them away.

Think about the businesses you recently walked into that made you feel welcome. What did the employees do that made you feel welcome? What aspects of the appearance of the business made you feel welcome?

_____

_____

_____

_____

Think about the businesses you recently walked into that made you feel uncomfortable. What did the employees do that made you feel uncomfortable? What aspects of the business' appearance made you feel uncomfortable?

_____
_____
_____
_____
_____

Remember that a customer's first impression is based on both the employees and the overall atmosphere of the company. A company can have a messy appearance and great employees. Likewise, a company may have a great appearance and employees with terrible attitudes. Apply the principles you learned in Part I, and you will help your customers form a favorable first impression.

 **PICTURE THIS**

Dave Benjamin has an appointment for a physical examination. He arrives at the physician's office, feeling slightly uneasy because it is his first appointment with this doctor. He walks into the office, looks around at bland beige walls, a row of uncomfortable looking chairs, a table with ripped magazines strewn about, and drab brown carpeting. Two other people are waiting. He eyes a sliding glass window with a note taped on it: Sign in, and we'll call you when we're ready for you. He signs his name on the pad and takes a seat. Someone on the other side of the window slides it open, looks at his name, and quickly shuts the window without saying a word. He sits, anxiously waiting and wondering when his name will be called.

The window slides open again. "Mr. Benjamin?"

Dave springs up and walks quickly to the window.

"You need to fill out this form since you haven't been here before," a woman says, no expression in her voice. "When you're done, ring the bell."

Dave takes the paper, fills it out, rings the bell, and sits back down. The woman slides the window open, takes the paper, and shuts the window without saying a word.

After the other two people are called, Dave waits for what seems an eternity. A nurse finally calls his name. "Mr. Benjamin?" He stands

and walks toward her. "Follow me. I need to weigh you and take your
blood pressure."

What Went Wrong?

Dave was always uncomfortable in a doctor's office. Being in this doctor's office
did nothing to ease his discomfort. No one made him feel welcome.

How Did the Customer Feel?

*How do you think the employees made Dave feel by the way they treated
him?*

_____

_____

_____

_____

What do you think was Dave's first impression of the doctor's office?

_____

_____

_____

_____

When you interact with customers face to face, presenting a positive business
personality means a lot. In other words, it is the complete package that counts.
Drab brown carpeting, bland beige walls, ripped magazines, and employees behind a glass wall say a lot about a business' personality. Imagine instead, if Dave
opened the door and saw a warm color scheme, an interesting mix of furniture
that looked comfortable and inviting, neatly arranged magazines, and an employee
who greeted him.

Focus, for a moment, on the image your company presents to your customers.
Take a mental walk through your business from a customer's viewpoint. Start by
walking through the front door. Take a good look at what your customers see
when they come into your business.

Doing the Walk Through

When you do your mental walk through, pretend you are seeing your business for the first time. Look at the colors, decorations, cleanliness, and neatness. How does your business look? Do you have an interesting focal point for your customers to see when they come in? How easy is it to move about? How accessible are your display areas? Is there a sensible traffic flow pattern? Is the lighting sufficient? Is everything clean, including bathrooms? Pay close attention to all details—your customers will.

What Can You Do to Improve the Look of Your Business?

As a group, try to come up with ideas to improve the overall look and image of your business. Think about color, function, and feel. Here are some things to pay attention to:

➜ Try to create a focal point for customers when they enter your business, such as an interesting piece of furniture, a piece of artwork, or an interesting display case. Create something that is memorable.

➜ Decorate your business in a style that suits the image you are trying to project. Knowing who your customers are is important when creating the appropriate look and feel for your business.

➜ Pay close attention to cleanliness and organization. Even if your business is decorated to suit your customers, it will not hold their attention if they first see clutter or a dirty appearance.

Now that you focused on your company's image, focus on your own. What image do you present to your customers when they walk into your business? Think about everything you learned in Chapters 1, 2, and 3. Think about the total package you present: your courtesies, attitude, appearance, manner of speaking, body language, listening skills, interaction, and overall interest.

Giving exceptional face-to-face customer service begins when you greet your customers. From the moment a customer walks into your business to the moment the customer leaves your business, you must take specific steps to make that customer feel important and valued.

Learn the following and you will be on your way to providing exceptional face-to-face customer service.

STEP 1: Saying Hello: Greeting the Customer
STEP 2: Between Hello and Goodbye: Helping the Customer
STEP 3: Saying Goodbye: Ending the Interaction

In Dave's situation, his discomfort would have been eased if he walked into an interesting, warm, and organized waiting room. He would have felt much better if the receptionist talked to him. When the nurse came for him, she could have smiled and made small talk to make him feel comfortable.

In answer to the questions, you may have written something like:

How do you think the employees made Dave feel by the way they treated him?
The employees did nothing to make him feel comfortable. Not saying hello and not talking to him about filling out the form probably made him feel even more uncomfortable. When the nurse came for him, she did nothing to put him at ease.

What do you think Dave's first impressions of the doctor's office were?
When he first came in and saw the drab appearance of the office, his first impression was not good. The doctor and the employees did not seem to care how the waiting room looked. The way the employees treated him did nothing to make him feel comfortable. He did not form a good first impression.

STEP 1: Saying Hello: Greeting the Customer

You learned in Chapter 1 how to make a good overall first impression, but there will be occasions when, no matter how hard you try, you do not make a good first impression. You might remind a customer of her old boyfriend. You might remind a customer of his rude neighbor. A customer might not like the way you look for no rational reason. When this happens, your first words will go a long way to start building your customer service foundation.

Greet every customer. A quick smile, an interested look, and a friendly greeting will show your customers that you are genuinely happy they came in to your business. Remember Kris in the gift shop? What a difference she and her coworkers made in the Final Take when they were interested in helping their customers. A friendly greeting will help overcome any negative vibes customers may have as they are forming their first impressions.

Make an impressionable opening statement. What you say is important in presenting yourself well to your customers. When you greet your customers, say more than hello. Add something to let them know you are happy they chose your business. Try something like: *"Hi, welcome to Karen's Bakery,"* or *"Hi, we're glad you came in."* When you say more than hello, your customers know you are interested in them and you appreciate that they chose your business. If you remember the customers from a previous visit, acknowledge them differently. Address them by name if you know it. *"It's great to see you again."* *"Hi Juanita, how are you doing today?"*

Ask, or say how you can provide help and give your name. After greeting your customers and making an impressionable opening statement , ask how you can help. Even if, like Sarah, your customers come in to browse, let them know you are there to help. You might say, *"Are you looking for anything particular to-day?"* or *"My name is Sarah, and I'll be happy to help you in any way."* In the doctor's office, the receptionist could have assured Dave she would help if he had any questions about the form. Since this was his first visit, talking to him would have helped put him at ease. *"Since this is your first visit with us, I'll need you to complete this patient information form. My name is Kathy and if you have any questions I'll be glad to answer them."*

Tune in to your customer. Pay close attention to your customer's body language. Watch for cues. Make eye contact, and smile at your customers. See how quickly and easily they smile back. Pick up on their attitudes. When you are interested in your customers, you will be able to pick up on their moods, and they will notice your interest. It was probably fairly evident that Dave was uncomfortable. *"Thank you for completing the form. You can have a seat, and the nurse will come for you. It shouldn't take long. We'll get you in as soon as possible."*

HOW COULD THE PHYSICIAN'S OFFICE STAFF GREET DAVE MORE POSITIVELY?

Dave Benjamin arrives at the physician's office, feeling slightly uneasy because it is his first appointment with this doctor. He walks into the office, looks around at warm gold walls, an interesting grouping of chairs, a table with magazines neatly organized, and an Oriental rug covering the wood floors.

He sees an open sliding glass window. A cheerful woman smiles and greets him. "Good morning, how are you today?"

"I'm fine, thank you. I'm Dave Benjamin. I have an appointment with Dr. Gilbert."

"Thank you. Mr. Benjamin, since this is your first time seeing Dr. Gilbert, will you please complete this new patient information form?" She reviews the form with Dave. "When you complete it, you can bring it back to me. My name is Kathy, and if you have any questions I'll be happy to help you." Sensing his discomfort, she smiles warmly.

Dave smiles back, completes the form, and returns it to Kathy.

She quickly looks it over. "Thanks Mr. Benjamin. Have a seat, and Dr. Gilbert's nurse will call you. It shouldn't take long."

When Kathy warmly greeted Dave, she gave him her full attention. She projected a confident, caring attitude that made Dave feel she was interested in him. Tuning in to his feelings, Kathy sensed he felt uneasy so she made it a point of offering to help him in any way she could and assuring him he would not have to wait long.

STEP 2: Between Hello and Goodbye: Helping the Customer

After greeting your customers, it is time to get to the nuts and bolts of helping them. They came to you for a reason. Finding out that reason and finding the best solution is your next step in helping your customers.

Pay attention to that one customer. And only that one customer. Show you are interested in helping by listening actively and making eye contact with the customer you are helping. Remember the employee at the deli? When he was helping Steve, he kept looking at the door whenever someone came in. Never do that when you are helping a customer. Looking at other people sends a clear message that those other people are more important than your customer.

Show and tell. When a customer asks where something is located, show the customer rather than pointing at or telling where it is. Walk the customer to that area of the store. If it is a small item, pick it up and hand it to the customer. If a customer asks about a product, tell him about it. Give a good description. Use your show-and-tell time to talk to the customer.

Make the most of your question and answer period. Refer back to Chapter 2, Step 4 and Chapter 3, Step 3. If the customer asks for a specific item, show the item to the customer and then ask questions to make sure it is the best solution. Use a combination of open and closed questions to learn more about what the customer needs. Make a recommendation based on what the customer tells you.

Know when to stay and when to go. Pick up on your customer's cues whether he wants you to stay and help or whether he wants to be left alone. Sometimes people come in to browse, or perhaps they are unsure what solution they are looking for. Do not be overbearing with customers. If they want time to look around, say, *"I'll be right here if I can help you,"* or *"I'll be happy to help if you need anything."*

If a phone call comes in while you are helping a customer, ask the caller to hold while you finish or offer to call back. Never make the customer, who is ready to do business, wait while you take a call.

HOW COULD DAVE'S VISIT TO THE DOCTOR HAVE GONE BETTER?

Soon a nurse comes into the waiting room. "Mr. Benjamin?" Dave stands and walks toward her. She smiles warmly. "My name is Ann. How are you doing?"

"I'm fine, thanks."

"Great. Come with me, I'll get you weighed and take your blood pressure first. Then Dr. Gilbert will see you."

By the time Ann came for him, Dave felt comfortable being in Dr. Gilbert's office. Both Kathy and Ann explained the procedures to Dave. Because Dave was comfortable with the employees, with the look of the office, and with the organized manner in which it was run, Dave felt he was in good hands.

What Steps Should You Take to Help Customers?

Discuss the steps you should take to help your customers. For example, in Dr. Gilbert's office, the employees are expected to make patients feel comfortable by being friendly and explaining every procedure. Review a typical customer interaction step by step. What, specifically, should you do to help your typical customer? It is important for you to know what you are expected to do to help your customers. Now you can give each customer the same level of service.

STEP 3: Saying Goodbye: Ending the Interaction

Customers are going to remember their visit to your company. Whether customers do business with you or not, why not make their visit memorable by making them feel valued?

Find the right solution. When you find the right solution for your customers, they will feel good about coming to you for help. Sometimes you will not have the best solution to offer, but even when you are not able to give them what they need, they will know that you tried your best.

Make sure the customer is satisfied. When you ask the correct questions and answer the questions correctly, when you identify the customer's needs, and when you find the best solution, go one step further to make sure the customer is satisfied with the solution. Say something like, *"I'm sure you'll be happy with that choice. It's one of our most popular items", "Do you have any questions about how this works?",* or *"I'm sorry we didn't have that doodah you were looking for."* Ask if you can help with anything else: *"Did you find everything you were looking for?", "Is there anything else I can help you find today?",* or *"Do you need batteries for this toy?"*

Thank customers for coming in to your business. Always let your customers know that you appreciate their business. If they do business with you say something such as, *"Enjoy your new. . . ."* or *"I'm glad I could resolve your billing problem."* If the customer does not do business with you say, *"Thanks for coming in,"* or *"Thanks. Next time I hope we have what you're looking for."* Let your customers know you hope to see them again: *"Please come back soon."*

HOW COULD THE STAFF AT DR. GILBERT'S OFFICE HAVE ENDED DAVE'S VISIT ON A POSITIVE NOTE?

Dr. Gilbert is finishing Dave's physical. "Mr. Benjamin, it looks like you are taking great care of yourself. Do you have any questions?"

"I can't think of any."

"All right. After you finish dressing, you can go to the reception area, and they'll finish your paperwork. Unless something comes up, I'll see you in a year. It was great meeting you." Dr. Gilbert smiles, shakes Dave's hand and says goodbye.

Kathy sees him coming. "Done already? I have your paperwork right here. Do you have any questions?"

"No, Dr. Gilbert was great. She spent a lot of time with me. I'm glad I came to see her."

"That's nice to hear. Would you like us to mail you a reminder card for your next appointment?"

"No, that's OK. I'll remember to call."

"We do get booked up quickly, so try to call about two months prior so we can get you a convenient appointment."

"Thanks for letting me know. I'll make sure I do that."

"Thank you for coming in and have a great day."

Kathy ended Dave's visit by asking if he had any questions. His answer told her he was satisfied with his interaction with Dr. Gilbert. She ended by thanking him for coming in.

The following week one of Dave's coworkers asked if anyone knew of a good doctor.

"I do. I just saw Dr. Gilbert last week for a physical. She was great. Besides that, the office is clean, the staff is very friendly, and they went out of their way to make me feel comfortable. I'd definitely recommend her."

Had Dave's visit ended with the Take One contact, chances are he would not be so quick to recommend Dr. Gilbert's office to his coworker.

Whenever you have your customer hat on and go into a business, pay close attention to the way you are treated. Think about the things you liked and the things you did not like. Learn from watching others. Make sure you treat customers the way you like to be treated.

PICTURE THIS

Dave Benjamin arrives at the physician's office, feeling slightly uneasy because it is his first appointment with this doctor. He walks in the office, looks around at warm gold walls, an interesting grouping of chairs, a table with magazines neatly organized, and an Oriental rug covering the wood floors.

He sees an open sliding glass window. A cheerful woman smiles and greets him. "Good morning, how are you today?"

"I'm fine, thank you. I'm Dave Benjamin. I have an appointment with Dr. Gilbert."

"Thank you. Mr. Benjamin, since this is your first time seeing Dr. Gilbert, will you please complete this new patient information form?" She reviews the form with Dave. "When you complete it, you can bring it back to me. My name is Kathy, and if you have any questions, I'll be happy to help you." Sensing his discomfort, she smiles warmly.

Dave smiles back, completes the form, and returns it to Kathy.

She quickly looks it over. "Thanks Mr. Benjamin. Have a seat, and Dr. Gilbert's nurse will call you. It shouldn't take long."

Soon a nurse comes into the waiting room. "Mr. Benjamin?" Dave stands and walks toward her. She smiles warmly. "My name is Ann. How are you doing?"

"I'm fine, thanks."

"Great. Come with me, I'll get you weighed and take your blood pressure first. Then Dr. Gilbert will see you."

Dr. Gilbert, upon finishing Dave's physical says, "Mr. Benjamin, it looks like you are taking great care of yourself. Do you have any questions?"

"I can't think of any."

"All right. After you finish dressing, you can go to the reception area, and they'll finish your paperwork. Unless something comes up, I'll see you in a year. It was great meeting you." Dr. Gilbert smiles, shakes Dave's hand and says goodbye.

Kathy sees him coming. "Done already? I have your paperwork right here. Do you have any questions?"

"No, Dr. Gilbert was great. She spent a lot of time with me. I'm glad I came to see her."

"That's nice to hear. Would you like us to mail you a reminder card for your next appointment?"

"No, that's OK. I'll remember to call."

"We do get booked up quickly, so try to call about two months prior so we can get you a convenient appointment."

"Thanks for letting me know. I'll make sure I do that."

"Great. Thanks for coming in and have a great day."

Although you may not automatically think of a physician's office as a customer service provider, think again. Every business provides customer service. It is important that anyone—in any business—who interacts with customers understands this. Customers, even patients, will go to someone else if they are not satisfied with their treatment.

Face-to-Face Contacts
KEY POINTS

STEP 1: Saying Hello: Greeting the Customer

Greet every customer

Make an impressionable opening statement

Ask or say how you can help and give your name

Tune in to your customer

STEP 2: Between Hello and Goodbye: Helping the Customer

Pay attention to the one customer

Show and tell

Make the most of your question-and-answer period

Know when to stay and when to go

STEP 3: Saying Goodbye: Ending the Interaction

Find the right solution

Make sure the customer is satisfied

Thank the customer for coming in to your business

Face-to-Face Contacts
PRACTICE LESSON

Refer to the customer contact example you noted at the beginning of the chapter.

STEP 1: Saying Hello: Greeting the Customer

What will you do when customers come in?

_____

_____

_____

_____

STEP 2: Between Hello and Goodbye: Helping the Customer

What general steps are you going to take to help your customer?

_____

_____

_____

_____

STEP 3: Saying Goodbye: Ending the Interaction

What will you do before the customer leaves your business?

_____

_____

_____

_____

What will you say to a customer for whom you could not find the right solution?

_____

_____

_____

_____

Think About . . .

Have **you** ever made customers feel uncomfortable being in your business?

Andrew recently moved and needed to open a new bank account. Three banks were in the area so he picked one at random. Walking in, he was greeted by gray: gray walls and gray carpet. Even the employees' personalities seemed to match the color scheme. No one looked at him. No one smiled.

Andrew sat down in a gray chair and waited for one of the account representatives to help him. As he waited, his discomfort grew. He looked around and thought, *I feel like I'm inside a battleship. What's up with the gray? And what's up with the employees? Everyone acts like they're robots.* Continuing to wait, he thought, *Maybe I'm invisible. I know they're all helping other people, but no one's even looked at me.*

Andrew left. He did not feel comfortable being there so he drove to another bank. He walked in, and one of the tellers greeted him: "Hello. Welcome to First Bank." Andrew explained to the teller he needed to open an account. The teller replied, "Everyone in new accounts is busy right now. Please have a seat, and someone will be with you shortly."

Andrew sat down in a comfortable chair and waited for an account representative. As he looked around, he noticed the bank was decorated tastefully, and he felt at ease. As he watched the employees, he saw that everyone seemed happy to be working at First Bank. Every time a customer came in, either one of the employees or the manager greeted the customer.

After opening his new account, Andrew stopped at the manager's desk and said, "Excuse me, I just want to tell you how nice it is to be in a place where the employees really seem to care about the customers."

The manager smiled, "Thank you for sharing that. Our policy is to make sure all our customers know that they are important to us. Every time you come in you can expect to be treated the same way."

Even with the dull gray color scheme and lackluster appearance, the employees at the other bank could have changed Andrew's poor first impression by being friendly and showing him that they valued his business. Had someone—anyone—greeted him and made him feel welcome, he would not have left.

Face-to-Face Contacts
QUICK QUOTES

Greet your customers when they walk through your door

Make your customers feel welcome

Smile and show enthusiasm for your work

When customers come into your business,
remember that they make your job possible

Keep a positive and friendly demeanor

Show, do not tell, where to find something

Tell your customers the benefits of your solution

Never take a personal phone call in the presence of customers

Never stand around looking bored; find something to keep you busy

When customers leave your business, thank them for coming in

CHAPTER 5

Saying It with a Smile: Telephone Contacts

SMILE WHEN TALKING ON THE PHONE. YOUR CUSTOMERS WILL *HEAR* YOUR SMILE THROUGH YOUR VOICE.

Write down a typical customer exchange that reflects your telephone contacts:

_____

_____

_____

_____

_____

_____

_____

_____

Think about this scenario as you work through this chapter. Use it as the example when answering the practice lesson questions.

Conducting business by telephone requires a different skill set than dealing with people face to face. Listening becomes even more important when you cannot see your customers. If you fail to listen, it is impossible to pick up on the nonverbal cues you get when you can see the other person.

When customers cannot see you, what you say, *how* you say it, and what you do not say are equally important. It is important to verbalize what you are doing. Silence, to a customer, can mean different things: *Are you still there?* or *What are you doing?* Answer your customers' silent questions before they ask them. *"I'm reading through the notes on my computer screen. It'll be just a moment."* Now the customer knows you are still there and you are working on the problem.

Maintaining a professional and friendly telephone demeanor, keeping an ongoing dialogue, asking appropriate questions, and responding appropriately to your customers are important skills to have when you interact with customers by phone.

 **PICTURE THIS**

Diane Parker likes the convenience of shopping by catalog. She sometimes orders over the Internet, but prefers calling because she likes interacting with a person. Ashley works in a catalog call center, where her job is to take orders from customers. She answers the following call from Diane:

"VeeJay's Sportswear."

"Hi, I'd like to place a catalog order."

"May I have your name and billing address?"

"Yes, Diane Parker. My address is 23 Sycamore Road. . . ."

"Is that the address to which you want your order shipped?"

"Yes."

"What is your first catalog number?"

"14236."

"Size?"

123

SAYING IT
WITH A
SMILE:
TELEPHONE
CONTACTS

"Medium."

"Color?"

"Rose."

"Next item?"

Diane continues to give her list of items, along with her credit card information. There is silence on the other end of the line. Diane waits. And waits. She begins to wonder what is happening. Has the employee put her on hold? Forgotten about her? Taken a break? "Hello," she says into the silence.

"I'm here," comes a bland reply. "I'm waiting for your order to process. It shouldn't be long."

Diane waits again.

"Your order has gone through. All items are in stock and will be shipped out tomorrow. Is there anything else I can help you with?"

"No thanks."

"Thank you for calling."

Diane hangs up, hoping the employee got all the items correct.

What Went Wrong?

Ashley was efficient in taking Diane's order. She most likely followed her company's expectations for handling catalog orders. But it sounded as though Diane was giving her order to an automated system. Ashley added nothing to her contact with Diane. Sophisticated call answering equipment could have taken the order just as well. While Ashley may have been efficient in taking the order, she left out the important detail of putting a personal touch into the contact. Putting a personal touch into your phone conversations will make you, as well as your company, come alive through the telephone.

How Did the Customer Feel?

How do you think Diane felt after she hung up from calling VeeJay's Sportswear? _____

_____

_____

_____

You already learned the importance of conveying a positive attitude through your body language and appearance when you deal with a customer in a face-to-face situation.

When you deal with customers on the telephone, your verbal communication skills, particularly your tone, are important. Your customers will "see" you through your voice, because they cannot see you through your appearance. Your attitude will come through the phone line, so whether your attitude is tinged with enthusiasm, sarcasm, boredom, or like Ashley, a robotic quality, your customer will hear you—loudly and clearly. Make sure the attitude you convey is a helpful and interested one.

Talking on the phone also requires greater listening ability, both on the customer's part and on your own. Focus on the customer you are helping rather than on the events happening around you. Be a complete listener. Never make a customer repeat a statement because you were not paying attention.

Learn the following steps and you will give exceptional customer service to your telephone customers.

STEP 1: Putting Your Best Ear Forward
STEP 2: Saying Hello: The Opener
STEP 3: Between Hello and Goodbye: Helping the Customer
STEP 4: Saying Goodbye: The Closer

In Diane's phone call, Ashley could have shown more enthusiasm by answering the call, *"Thank you for calling VeeJay's. How can I help you today?"* She could have interacted more throughout the contact. For example, she could have repeated the item name when Diane gave the number, *"Item 14236, the denim jacket. What size and color would you like that in?"* Small verbalizations like these can make a big difference with customers. Diane would have had instant confirmation that her items were ordered correctly.

In answer to the question, you may have answered something like:

How do you think Diane felt after she hung up from calling VeeJay's Sportswear?

125

SAYING IT
WITH A
SMILE:
TELEPHONE
CONTACTS

The employee did nothing to establish rapport. Diane did not feel comfortable with their interaction and she hoped the employee input her order correctly.

STEP 1: Putting Your Best Ear Forward

When you communicate with another person face to face, it can be fairly easy to fudge when you do not listen completely. You can pick up cues by paying attention to a person's body language. You can drift off and be able to pick up somewhere in the middle of the conversation and go with the flow by watching the other person's actions as he or she speaks. Not so when you are on the phone. When you cannot see the other person, your only means of communication is the give and take of listening and talking. When you do not listen effectively, it can be pretty tough to respond effectively. When you handle customers by telephone, listen, listen, listen.

Review Chapter 2, Step 6. Focus entirely on your customer. Listen completely. Remain objective; do not judge. Even though it will be difficult for you to listen for what is not said when you cannot see the other person, you will be able to hear a person's attitude and emotions by listening carefully to the voice tone.

Listen to the customer's opening statement. The first words out of the customer's mouth tell you the reason for the call. Never let the first words out of your mouth be to ask your customer to repeat his opening statement because you were not giving your full attention.

Write down or input key points. Have pen and paper ready or have the correct computer screen displayed when you take a call. If the customer gives you his or her name, write it down. If the customer seems upset, write down the main points of the opening statement, for example, *Mrs. Brennan—received wrong color jacket—got blue, wanted white.* You do not have to write verbatim, just highlight the key points.

Listen without interrupting. If Mrs. Brennan is telling you why she is calling and you interrupt her midsentence, she is not going to be very happy: *"This is Mrs. Brennan. I just received my order and one of the items. . . ."* *"Hold on just a second Mrs. Brennan, I'm finishing up an order. As soon as my screen clears, I'll be able to help you."* If Mrs. Brennan was not upset when she called, she most likely would be when the employee interrupted her and was not ready to help. Even if the computer screen needed to clear, the employee could have listened and jotted down the key points.

Give the customer you are helping your full attention. For example: *"This is Mrs. Brennan. I just received my order and one of the items isn't what I ordered."*

127

SAYING IT
WITH A
SMILE:
TELEPHONE
CONTACTS

"What is your name?" *"Mrs. Brennan."* *"You said you received an order?"* What happened here? Because this employee did not listen, Mrs. Brennan is going to have to say it all over again. How do you think she will feel if she has to repeat what she just said because the employee was not paying attention? Once you understand the reason for the call, follow your company guidelines to fulfill the request.

STEP 2: Saying Hello: The Opener

Now that we reviewed and recovered the importance of listening, starting with the customer's opening statement, we can begin the call process.

Answer on the first ring. Customers expect a business line to be answered on the first, and no later than the second, ring. After that, they may hang up. Once they hang up, you may have lost a potential customer.

Give the name of your business, your name, and then an opening statement or question. When giving your opening question or statement, sound like you really want to help the caller. Answer in a professional, yet friendly tone. You can sound professional—and—friendly at the same time. With practice, you can manage the balance between sounding too mechanical or overly friendly.

Sound enthusiastic and ready to help. Project enthusiasm and eagerness to help in your telephone voice. Listen closely to your customer's opening statement and respond accordingly. Never make a customer repeat information because you failed to listen or because you were not prepared to make note of his request.

Work on relationship building from the beginning of the contact. Make a good first impression by speaking in a friendly voice that conveys a willingness to help. Establish a rapport by finding common ground. Address the customer by name if you know it.

Addressing the Customer by Name

It is generally all right to use the customer's first name if that is the introduction provided. Use good judgment on this and, when in doubt, address the customer using Mr., Mrs., or Ms. and the last name. Let the customer be the one to let you know if it is all right to use a first name.

→ What are your company's expectations for addressing customers?

→ Does management prefer a more formal or a more casual greeting?

129

SAYING IT
WITH A
SMILE:
TELEPHONE
CONTACTS

When speaking on the phone, with customers, fellow workers, or other business contacts, never chew gum or eat. You might think the person on the other end does not hear, but you may be wrong.

HOW COULD ASHLEY START HER PHONE CONTACT IN A MORE POSITIVE MANNER?

"Thank you for calling VeeJay's Sportswear. My name is Ashley. How may I help you today?"

Ashley answered the call on the first ring. She gave the name of the business, her name, and asked how she could help. Her enthusiasm and willingness to help came through to Diane.

STEP 3: Between Hello and Goodbye: Helping the Customer

Between hello and goodbye, you have the opportunity to handle your customer's request in a manner that leaves her feeling good about calling your company. You can also handle your customer's request in a manner that leaves her wondering why she bothered calling. You are your company's voice; how you handle your customer's request by telephone is how the customer is going to remember your company. Be sure you represent it well.

Assure the customer you can help. Respond to your customer's opening statement with an assurance that you can help. Say something like, *"Absolutely. I can help you with that."* Even if you are going to refer the customer to another department or employee, you can give an assurance. Say, *"I'm going to transfer you to the department that can take care of this for you, but I will stay on the line until someone answers."*

Summarize the customer's opening statement. Before you attempt to handle a customer's request, make sure you understand what the customer wants. Recap what the customer said without repeating it verbatim. In Mrs. Brennan's call you could say, *"You received your order, but we sent you a blue jacket instead of white?"* This way the customer will clear up any confusion before you go on, *"No, I received a white jacket but I wanted blue."* If it is a short request, such as Diane's call to place an order, incorporate the summary into your assurance statement, *"I'll be happy to take your catalog order."*

Verbalize what you are doing. Tell your customer what you are doing throughout the contact. Never assume the person on the other end understands. During silences, the customer may be wondering if you are still there. This does not mean you need to constantly chatter your way through the contact, but you should tell your customer what you are doing to help. If you need to ask a series of questions to help, explain what you will be doing so the customer does not think you are interrogating, *"Mrs. Brennan, I'm going to need some additional information to help you. Do you have your invoice handy?"* Now when you begin asking questions, Mrs. Brennan understands what you are doing.

Put your personal touch into the contact. You can maintain professionalism but show your human side. Talk to the customer while you are waiting for a computer screen to change, *"It'll be just a moment for the next screen. How are*

131

SAYING IT
WITH A
SMILE:
TELEPHONE
CONTACTS

you doing today?" If a customer asks you to do something you are unsure of, say so. Follow up with, *"I'll check with my supervisor. I want to make sure I handle this correctly."*

If you are a new employee, it is all right to say so. Everyone has been new at a job, and customers will not only relate but will appreciate your honesty. You can explain, *"I appreciate your patience. I'm new and I want to make sure I input everything correctly for you."*

Now is a good time to make sure you are completely familiar with your company's procedures and policies. Ask yourself: Have I been trained to do my job? Do I have the necessary tools to work effectively and efficiently? If not, tell your manager what training you need. Keep up to date on changes in your workplace by asking questions to learn more about your job and your company.

Before a lengthy pause, tell the customer what is happening. There are many instances in which you will need to pause the conversation. For example, you might need to wait for the order to process, wait for another computer screen to come up, read notes from previous contacts, or are a new employee and not working up to speed yet. Let the customer know why you are pausing the conversation. This will avoid awkward silences. You can say, *"It'll take a moment for the order to process. Then I can give you a confirmation number. I'll be on the line with you, though."*

When putting customers on hold, explain why. This is a common courtesy your customers will appreciate, *"Mrs. Brennan, I'm going to put you on hold so I can see what happened with your order."* In addition, tell your customer approximately how long it will take, *"It may take me a few minutes to get the information I need to help you."* If you put a customer on hold and then find it is taking longer than you thought, return to the line to give an update, *"Mr. Perkins, I'm still waiting for my technician to give me an answer. It shouldn't take that much longer."* When you come back to the line, thank the customer for waiting, *"Mr. Perkins, thank you for holding. The technician explained. . . ."*

If the wait time will be extremely long, offer a call back. Always make a specific commitment. Say, *"I'll get back to you by five today with the information,"* rather than *"I'll call you back as soon as possible."* As soon as possible may mean one time frame to you, an entirely different time frame to your customers.

Outgoing Telephone Contacts

If your job requires you to make outgoing phone contacts, come up with an outline for handling these type calls. Include:

➔ Greeting—introduce yourself and your company

➔ Explain the reason for your call up front

➔ Know what you are going to say before you call

➔ Practice your message before calling

If your company makes cold calls for sales, come up with a framework for the dialogue you will use. Practice by role playing the contact before you actually make a call.

HOW COULD ASHLEY HELP DIANE MORE EFFECTIVELY?

"Hi, I'd like to place a catalog order."

"I'll be glad to take your order. May I have your name and your billing address?"

"Sure. It's Diane Parker. My address is 23 Sycamore Road. . . ."

"Is that the address to which you want your order shipped?"

"Yes."

"It'll take just a minute for my screen to change. How are you doing today?"

133

SAYING IT
WITH A
SMILE:
TELEPHONE
CONTACTS

"I'm great, how are you?"

"I'm doing great, too. Hmm, our system seems to be a little slow this morning, but the screen should come right up." After a short pause, Ashley says, "Here we go. I'm ready to take your order now. What is your first catalog number?"

"SU—14236."

"That's the misses denim jacket. What size and color would you like that?"

"Size medium in rose."

"I have the same jacket, and it's really comfortable. What is the next item number?"

"SU—14707."

"Denim slacks. Size and color?"

"Size ten in rose."

"All right. Next?"

Ashley takes all the information, adding a personal touch from time to time until Diane finishes.

"Thank you. It'll take a moment for the order to process and then I'll give you your confirmation number."

Ashley assured Diane she could help and summarized the reason for the call. She verbalized what she was doing throughout the contact and before pauses she explained the reason. She built a relationship throughout the contact by being friendly, yet professional.

STEP 4: Saying Goodbye: The Closer

Learning how to effectively handle customer contacts by telephone begins when you answer, continues when you take care of the customer's request, and ends when you say goodbye. Remember, telephone customers are going to judge your company by their interactions with you. Ending the call effectively will make your customers feel good that they did business with your company.

Recap what you are going to do. When you have finished handling the customer's request, end the contact on a positive note by assuring the customer that you either have or will handle the request. Say something like, *"Mr. Downs, I have issued a credit for the finance charge."* In the case of a lengthy request, it is not necessary to recap each item. You could say, *"Mr. Downs, I've issued a credit and noted your account of the other items we discussed."*

Gain the customer's acceptance. When you recap, the customer knows exactly what you will be doing. Wait for the customer's acknowledgment and acceptance to make sure you handled everything correctly. If you recapped incorrectly, the customer will let you know. Doing this will cut down on errors and will ultimately increase customer satisfaction.

Ask if you can help with anything else. This is another way to show your human touch and also a nice way to end the contact. Asking this simple question gives your customers a chance to pause and think before hanging up. They will appreciate the memory jogger.

Give your name again. Let the customer know you will be happy to help if she needs to call back. Say something like:, *"My name is Ashley, and if you need anything else I'll be glad to help you with it."* If you work in a large call center that would make it difficult for the customer to reach you personally, say: *"My name is Ashley. Your order has been processed. I'll give you the confirmation number as soon as it comes up. If you need to call back anyone can access your order either by the confirmation number or by your name and address."*

Thank the customer for calling your business. Always end on a positive note, *"Thank you for calling (name) Company. Have a great day."*

135

SAYING IT
WITH A
SMILE:
TELEPHONE
CONTACTS

HOW COULD ASHLEY END THE CONTACT MORE EFFECTIVELY?

After a short pause, Ashley says, "Mrs. Parker, your order for the five items has been processed. Everything is in stock and will be shipped out tomorrow. Do you have a pen and paper handy so I can give you your confirmation number?"

"Yes."

"The number is 061524."

"OK. Great."

"Is there anything else I can help you with today?"

"No, I think that should do it."

"Again, my name is Ashley. If you need to call back regarding your order anyone here can reference it by the confirmation number or by your name and address. Thank you for calling VeeJay's and have a great day."

"Thank you."

Because the order was lengthy, Ashley recapped the total number of items. She waited for Diane's acceptance, then asked if she could help with anything else. She completed the call by giving her name and thanking Diane for calling.

 **PICTURE THIS**

"Thank you for calling VeeJay's Sportswear. My name is Ashley. How may I help you today?"

"Hi, I'd like to place a catalog order."

"I'll be glad to take your order. May I have your name and your billing address?"

"Sure. It's Diane Parker. My address is 23 Sycamore Road. . . ."

"Is that the address to which you want your order shipped?"

"Yes."

"It'll take just a minute for my screen to change. How are you doing today?"

"I'm great, how are you?"

"I'm doing great, too. Hmm, our system seems to be a little slow this morning, but the screen should come right up." After a short pause, Ashley says, "Here we go. I'm ready to take your order now. What is your first catalog number?"

"SU—14236."

"That's the misses denim jacket. What size and color would you like that?"

"Size medium in rose."

"I have the same jacket, and it's really comfortable. What is the next item number?"

"SU—14707."

"Denim slacks. Size and color?"

"Size ten in rose."

"All right. Next?"

Ashley takes all the information, adding a personal touch from time to time until Diane finishes.

"Thank you. It'll take a moment for the order to process and then I'll give you your confirmation number."

After a short pause, Ashley says, "Mrs. Parker, your order for the five items has been processed. Everything is in stock and will be shipped out tomorrow. Do you have a pen and paper handy so I can give you your confirmation number?"

"Yes."

"The number is 061524."

"OK. Great."

"Is there anything else I can help you with today?"

"No, I think that should do it."

"Again, my name is Ashley. If you need to call back regarding your order anyone here can reference it by the confirmation number or by your name and address. Thank you for calling VeeJay's and have a great day."

"Thank you."

The right combination to satisfying customers is to know what to do, do it right, and do it with enthusiasm and a desire to help.

137

SAYING IT
WITH A
SMILE:
TELEPHONE
CONTACTS

Telephone Contacts
KEY POINTS

STEP 1: Putting Your Best Ear Forward

Listen to the customer's opening statement

Write down or input key points

Listen without interrupting

Give the customer you are helping your full attention

STEP 2: Saying Hello: The Opener

Answer on the first ring

Give the name of your business, your name, and an opening statement or question

Sound enthusiastic and ready to help

Work on relationship building from the beginning of the contact

STEP 3: Between Hello and Goodbye: Helping the Customer

Assure the customer you can help

Summarize the customer's opening statement

Verbalize what you are doing

Put your personal touch into the contact

Before a lengthy pause, tell the customer what is happening

When putting customers on hold, explain why

STEP 4: Saying Goodbye: The Closer

Recap what you are going to do

Gain the customer's acceptance

Ask if you can help with anything else

Give your name again

Thank the customer for calling your business

Telephone Contacts
PRACTICE LESSON

STEP 1: Putting Your Best Ear Forward

Write down some things you can do to be a better listener on the telephone.

_____

_____

_____

_____

Refer to the customer contact example you noted at the beginning of the chapter.

STEP 2: Saying Hello: The Opener

Write down how you will greet your customer.

_____

_____

_____

_____

STEP 3: Between Hello and Goodbye: Helping the Customer

Assure the customer you can help. Summarize the customer's opening statement.

_____

_____

_____

_____

What are some ways you can verbalize what you are doing?

_____

_____

_____

_____

139

SAYING IT
WITH A
SMILE:
TELEPHONE
CONTACTS

Write down what you might say when there is a pause on the line. Write down what you might say before putting a customer on hold.

_____

_____

_____

_____

STEP 4: Saying Goodbye: The Closer

Recap how you going to handle the customer's request.

_____

_____

_____

_____

How will you end the contact? (Remember to ask if you can help with anything else, give your name again, and thank the customer for calling your business).

_____

_____

_____

_____

Think About . . .

Have **you** ever been guilty of not listening to your telephone customers?

Sean called the telephone company to establish new local service. The representative was friendly, but she appeared preoccupied. Twice during the contact Sean told the employee that he was not moving until the following month and did not want service to begin until then.

"We can install your phone service next Tuesday."

"No. Remember, I told you I don't want my service to start until September 23. I'm remodeling the home and that's the date I'll be moving into it."

"Oh, that's right. You did tell me that. . . ."

After spending nearly an hour setting up his new phone service, Sean did not feel completely comfortable when he hung up. *I just know something is going to go wrong,* he thought.

Two weeks later Sean received a phone bill for his new service. The date the service began was the Tuesday the representative first offered him. He was not surprised, but he was upset.

The employee's mistake cost him one more hour on the telephone straightening the mess out. Had the representative given him her full attention, this would not have happened. By the time he finished the second call, Sean had little confidence in the company.

141

SAYING IT
WITH A
SMILE:
TELEPHONE
CONTACTS

Telephone Contacts
QUICK QUOTES

Answer the phone on the first ring

Listen closely to the customer's opening statement

Allow the customer to speak without interruption

Establish your credibility by assuring your customer you can help

Your attitude comes through the phone lines; make yours a positive one

Give the customer your full attention

If the hold time will be long, offer to call back within a specific time frame

Build rapport throughout the contact by talking to your customer

Vocalize your responses so your customer will know what you are doing

Thank your customer for calling the business

CHAPTER 6

Looking Before You Leap: E-commerce Contacts

Write down a typical customer contact that is reflective of your E-commerce interactions:

_____

_____

_____

_____

_____

_____

_____

_____

Think about this scenario as you work through this chapter. Use it as the example when answering the practice lesson questions.

E-commerce has grown exponentially in the past few years. Customers, who only a few years ago were leery of conducting business over the Internet, now do so with ease. Customers find it simple and convenient to do business online, as long as they feel the company is reputable. Consumers' growing comfort level with the Internet has opened up the global market faster than any other medium. We now have virtually unlimited options.

When conducting E-commerce, communication requires yet another skill set. Communication, primarily handled through E-mail, is a great way to formulate thoughts, but you must take special care to make sure that what you write is what you mean to write. Learning to write well by formulating your thoughts clearly and conveying the correct message is the most important skill for E-commerce customer service contacts.

PICTURE THIS

Mr. Bowman is interested in buying a new set of golf clubs, so he surfed the Internet for information. He used a key word search and one of the Web sites he checked offers the set he wants at a good price. He is unclear about shipping charges and sends an E-mail query. Tom, an employee at the sporting goods store, replies to Mr. Bowman's E-mail by writing the following:

> The shipping charges to send the set of golf clubs you inquired about will be $3.00.
> Nineteenth Hole Golf Company

Tom hits the send button. Later he is reviewing the E-mail and reads—$3.00. He meant to type $30.00. Small mistake. Costly difference. How is Mr. Bowman going to feel if he places his order and finds out he was quoted the wrong shipping charges?

What Went Wrong?

Tom was hasty in hitting the send button without proofreading the E-mail. If the customer places an order, Tom and his company have two options: either eat the

145

LOOKING
BEFORE
YOU LEAP:
E-COMMERCE
CONTACTS

cost of shipping or E-mail the customer with the correct quote. Neither of these options is ideal. For a small company, eating the difference in the cost of shipping can quickly cut into its profit margin. Telling the customer he was quoted an incorrect rate can cause the customer to lose faith in the company. It can cost the company a sale and a potential future customer relationship.

Valuing your E-prospects and giving them exceptional service online can turn prospective buyers into loyal customers. Customers who interact with a business over the Internet deserve the same level of customer service as face-to-face and telephone customers.

Master the following steps and you will be able to handle any E-customer in any E-situation.

> **STEP 1: What Does the E-Customer Expect?**
> **STEP 2: Hanging the Open Sign: Being Accessible**
> **STEP 3: Writing What You Mean: E-mail Communication**
> **STEP 4: Speaking Around the World: Cross-Cultural Etiquette**

In the contact between Tom and Mr. Bowman, had Tom carefully read the E-mail before hitting the send button, he might have caught and corrected the mistake. Now he is caught in a dilemma.

Before we go into E-commerce customer service, we need to discuss Web sites. Many companies now have a Web site. How your company's Web site is designed can make the difference between increased sales and frustrated surfers. As a group, review your Web site from a customer's viewpoint.

Building a Winning Web Site

The most important factor when building a Web site is to make it easy for your customers to navigate. Slow response times, complicated order blanks, and busy or confusing pages can easily turn a potential customer away. The best way to determine how your customers navigate through your site is to check it out yourself.

Pretend you know nothing about your company. Navigate your site as though you are a potential customer. Place a dummy order. Make note of the aspects of your site that are good and the aspects that need improvement.

Things to help you build a winning Web site:

→ Keep text to a minimum. In general, people prefer nonbusy pages when reading computer screens.

→ When using photos or other graphics, make sure they do not grind the surfing pace to a halt.

→ Make sure ordering is easy by monitoring the product information page, shopping cart, customer registration, billing information, and final checkout.

→ Include warranty or guarantee information and information about technical support, if appropriate, on your site.

→ Include a "contact the company" button for easy E-mailing.

→ Select words and phrases customers are likely to use for key word searches.

147

LOOKING
BEFORE
YOU LEAP:
E-COMMERCE
CONTACTS

STEP 1: What Does the E-customer Expect?

The E-customer can be anybody from anywhere. When you do business over the Internet, you open your door to customers around the globe. Customers who transact business over the Internet put their blind faith in your company. They deserve the same level of customer service you give your local customers.

When they enter your E-business, your potential customers have no idea what your business looks like. They cannot tell if your company is a multimillion dollar corporation or a small business run out of a home or a strip mall location. No matter how large or small your company is, it is important that you handle all your E-customers with professionalism and courtesy.

What are your customers looking for?

They want to know you are legitimate. Your home page is your customer's first step into your door. How your "door step" is laid out can either invite customers in or make them go elsewhere. Tell customers, up front, that you are a legitimate company and that you stand behind your products. Explain your service and product guarantees on your home page, if possible. By telling your customers that you care enough about them to guarantee their satisfaction, you are telling them that you value them as customers. Reiterate this in all E-mail correspondence.

They want to know you are trustworthy. You show you are trustworthy by the way you interact with your customers. Promptly answer all customer E-mail queries. When customers place orders, send detailed order confirmation E-mails. When you demonstrate to customers you are reliable and informative by responding quickly and effectively through E-communication, they will be more comfortable placing their trust in you and your company.

They want to know you will do what you say you will when you say you will. When customers ask questions, respond to their E-mails promptly. When they place orders, get them out quickly. Do not make your E-customers wait longer than if they came in to your business to buy something. If a customer sends you an E-mail query and you take a week to answer it or answer it in a haphazard manner, you do not look very reputable. If it takes so long to send an E-mail, how long will it take to process an order or handle a problem? Responding to E-mail queries promptly shows you are interested in your E-customers.

They want to know you have a human touch. When customers E-mail you for information, always put a human touch in your replies. Imagine you are communicating with a customer who is in your business. Let your personality come through in your E-mails by being responsive, friendly, and professional.

HOW COULD TOM HAVE BEEN MORE EFFECTIVE IN HIS RESPONSE?

Tom's initial reply to Mr. Bowman looked as though it was stock text that he copied into the E-mail. Now Tom responds differently.

> The shipping charges to send the complete set will be $30.00. We stand behind all our equipment. Your satisfaction is always guaranteed.
> We look forward to hearing from you and doing business with you.
>
> Sincerely,
> Nineteenth Hole Golf Company

This E-mail is an improvement over the first because Tom added a human touch in the text by showing his interest in doing business with Mr. Bowman. He clearly told Mr. Bowman that his satisfaction is guaranteed, which lends legitimacy to the company.

What's in a Name?

Unless your company is an easily recognized name, customers will find you by doing a key word search on a search engine. Come up with words and phrases your customers are most likely to use to find your business.

149

LOOKING
BEFORE
YOU LEAP:
E-COMMERCE
CONTACTS

STEP 2: Hanging the Open Sign: Being Accessible

Wthen you conduct business over the Internet, customers feel welcome to come in to your business twenty-four hours a day. When you do business over the Internet, you have no office hours, so it is important for you to be accessible to your customers. Remember, your E-customers do not know a one-person operation from a business that employs thousands.

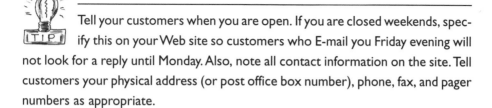

Tell your customers when you are open. If you are closed weekends, specify this on your Web site so customers who E-mail you Friday evening will not look for a reply until Monday. Also, note all contact information on the site. Tell customers your physical address (or post office box number), phone, fax, and pager numbers as appropriate.

Respond to E-customers quickly. You build credibility as a company by being responsive to all your customers. Give your E-customers the same importance as if they were in your business looking at you. Thank the customer for his interest in your company and products. Anticipate other questions the customer may have and address them in your E-mail. In other words, give more than is asked for. For example, Tom could have added information about order processing and shipping schedules in his E-mail to Mr. Bowman. Not only would this have added a human touch; it would have provided Mr. Bowman with the additional information that could have clinched the sale.

Process orders quickly. When customers do business over the Internet they want to know their orders will be quickly processed. When an order has been shipped, send a confirmation E-mail. Thank the customer for the order, summarize what was shipped, when it was shipped, and provide tracking information. When an item is backordered, let the customer know the approximate shipping date. Assure the customer you will not bill his or her credit card until the item is shipped and give an option if he or she does not want to proceed with the order.

Build customer loyalty through E-mailing. Always thank customers for their interest in your company. Use E-mails to tell customers about sales, special discounts, or new products. Send information to your repeat customers to let them know what is happening in your business. Always include an opt-out for those customers who do not want to receive unsolicited E-mails. If you deal with the same E-customers repeatedly, keep in contact with them through *thinking of you* or *how are you doing* E-mails. Keeping your company's name in the customers' minds not only can generate additional sales, it tells your customers you value their business.

HOW COULD TOM HAVE BEEN MORE EFFECTIVE IN HIS RESPONSE?

Thank you for your interest in the Magnum-18 Golf Clubs. The shipping charges to send the complete set will be $30.00. All in-stock items are shipped by the following business day. We are closed weekends, so any orders placed on Friday will be shipped the following Monday.

We stand behind all our equipment. **Your satisfaction is always guaranteed.**

We look forward to hearing from you. If you would like to be informed about special sales, please respond to this E-mail, and I will be happy to add you to our E-mail list.

Sincerely,
Nineteenth Hole Golf Company

Tom thanked Mr. Bowman for his interest in his company's products. He provided ordering and shipping information and included information for Mr. Bowman to sign up for notification of sales.

151

LOOKING
BEFORE
YOU LEAP:
E-COMMERCE
CONTACTS

STEP 3: Writing What You Mean: E-mail Communication

By now, Tom's E-mail sounds much better than his first one. As you saw, it is easy to make a mistake when typing is your means of communication. Chances for miscommunication increase when you type rather than speak your answer.

When E-mail is your means of communicating with your customers, you want to make sure that what you write is what you mean to write. Take special care before hitting the send button.

Use good communication skills. Begin with your subject line. Make sure it reflects the content of your E-mail. For example, *Order Confirmation* tells your customer exactly what she will be reading when she opens the E-mail. In the body of the letter, interject words like *yes, I'll be happy to take care of that, absolutely,* or *I've taken care of that for you.* Using the same words in E-mails that you use in oral communication lets your personality come through. Writing *Thank you for doing business. . . .* or *We appreciate your business. . . .* lets your company's personality come through as well.

Begin with a salutation. Begin your E-mails with a personal touch: *Dear Mr. Bowman. . . .* Mr. Bowman knows the E-mail is directed to him specifically. If you do not know the name, begin with a generic salutation reflective of your business, such as *Greetings from Nineteenth Hole Golf Company* or *Dear Fellow Golfer.*

Make messages visually interesting. Keep your messages short. When customers see a long block of print, chances are they are going to skip over parts of the message. Use short sentences and action verbs to express yourself: *We shipped your order. . . .* rather than *The order was shipped. . . .* Use short paragraphs and double spacing between them to create open space in the body of your messages. Use bullets or headings when possible.

Write as you would say it. If you are unsure of your wording, speak the message out loud to hear how it sounds. Put the most important items first. Write clearly and specifically. Do not depend solely on your computer's spellcheck to spot misspellings. Carefully proofread all messages. Keep the shortcut lingo (lol, jk, etc.) for your friends, not your business customers. Reread all E-mail messages before hitting the send button.

Add an interesting closing. Say something specific. This is a good place to interject your company's personality by adding a line to show your customer you value the business. Always sign with your name and title, rather than only your title or the name of your business.

ONE MORE TIME: HOW COULD TOM HAVE BEEN MORE EFFECTIVE IN HIS RESPONSE?

Dear Mr. Bowman,

Thank you for your interest in the Magnum-18 Golf Clubs. This is our most popular set of clubs and a great choice. The shipping charges to send the complete set will be $30.00. I will be happy to take your order and answer any additional questions you may have.

❖ We ship all in-stock items by the following business day.
❖ We are closed weekends so any orders placed on Friday will be shipped the following Monday.
❖ We stand behind all our equipment. **Your satisfaction is always guaranteed.**

We look forward to hearing from you. If you would like to be informed about special sales, please respond to this E-mail; in the subject line type "add to list."

At Nineteenth Hole Golf Company we appreciate your business. Our customers always start on the first hole.

Sincerely,
Tom Campbell
Golf Sales Consultant

In this E-mail, Tom began by addressing Mr. Bowman by name. He answered Mr. Bowman's question first, interjected his personality by saying that this was a great choice, and said he will be happy to help with future needs. He used easy-to-understand words, kept paragraphs short, and used bullets to highlight company

153

LOOKING
BEFORE
YOU LEAP:
E-COMMERCE
CONTACTS

policies. Throughout the message, Tom used good communication skills. He included a phrase that reflects his company's attitude toward its customers. He ended with a good closing that included his name and title.

Mr. Bowman was impressed by Tom's quick response and detailed E-mail. He had enough trust in Nineteenth Hole to place his order. After it was shipped, Tom sent a confirming E-mail.

Mr. Bowman,

We shipped your order today for the following item:

❖ Magnum-18 Golf Club Complete Set

Our customers give us great feedback on these clubs, and I'm sure you'll enjoy using them. If you have any questions, please feel free to E-mail or call me. I will be glad to help you with any future needs.

Thank you for your order. At Nineteenth Hole Golf Company, we appreciate your business.

Sincerely,
Tom Campbell
Golf Sales Consultant

STEP 4: Speaking Around the World: Cross-Cultural Etiquette

We live in a world made up of many cultures, customs, and languages. The Internet has shrunk our world so much that it is important to learn how to speak around the globe. Even though we may speak different languages, some communication skills are universal. Did you know there is a version of the Golden Rule in every culture? The words, depending on the origin, are different from those we learned as children, but the meaning is the same.

Treat other people as you want to be treated. The following qualities translate into every language: showing respect, being considerate of others, having a helpful attitude, using basic courtesies, displaying compassion and empathy for others, and treating people as individuals. When you do these things, you can learn to effectively communicate across language or cultural barriers.

Read carefully so you will "listen" well. People may write in a way that makes it difficult for you to understand the message when you first read it. When you receive an E-mail that is not clear, reread it carefully word for word to make sure you understand the meaning correctly.

Use correct grammar. Your E-customers may not understand jargon or slang. When you get in the habit of using correct grammar every time you speak and write, people will better understand your message. Do not try to mimic other peoples' manner of speaking. Be yourself and speak and write in your normal voice, but be mindful that language differences may hamper communication effectiveness.

Be a professional. You show you are a professional by not stereotyping other people, not talking down to others, and not making assumptions. When you treat other people with dignity, you show that you are respectful and tolerant. Always be professional in your responses and give a complete explanation of any words or terms your E-customer might not understand.

155

LOOKING
BEFORE
YOU LEAP:
E-COMMERCE
CONTACTS

E-commerce Contacts
KEY POINTS

STEP 1: What Does the E-customer Expect?

They want to know you are legitimate

They want to know you are trustworthy

They want to know you will do what you say you will when you say you will

They want to know you have a human touch

STEP 2: Hanging the Open Sign: Being Accessible

Respond to E-customers quickly

Process orders quickly

Build customer loyalty through E-mailing

STEP 3: Writing What You Mean: E-mail Communication

Use good communication skills

Begin with a salutation

Make messages visually interesting

Write as you would say it

Add an interesting closing

STEP 4: Speaking Around the World: Cross-Cultural Etiquette

Treat other people as you want to be treated

Read carefully so you will "listen" well

Use proper grammar

Be a professional

E-commerce Contacts
PRACTICE LESSON

STEP 1: What Does the E-customer Expect?
Write down some things that are important to E-customers.

_____
_____
_____
_____

STEP 2: Hanging the Open Sign: Being Accessible
What are some things your company can do on its Web site to show your E-customers you are accessible?

_____
_____
_____
_____

Refer to the customer contact example you noted at the beginning of the chapter.

STEP 3: Writing What You Mean: E-mail Communication
Write down a typical E-mail request you might receive from a customer.

_____
_____
_____
_____

Now write a response to the customer.

_____
_____
_____
_____

157

LOOKING
BEFORE
YOU LEAP:
E-COMMERCE
CONTACTS

STEP 4: Speaking Around the World: Cross-Cultural Etiquette

What are some things you can do to better communicate with people from other countries?

_____

_____

_____

_____

Think About . . .

Have **you** ever caused an E-customer to lose trust in you?

Lori needed to purchase a gift for a wedding. She knew the bride's china pattern and thought it would be convenient to place her order online. She did a word search for the pattern, chose a company at random, and found what she wanted on the site.

The items were priced reasonably, but Lori wanted to know if they were in stock before placing her order. She E-mailed the company and waited for an answer. After two days without any response, she again searched the Internet for another company, choosing another one at random. She found the items she was interested in purchasing. This company also had a current listing of in-stock pieces, so Lori had immediate confirmation that her items were in stock and would be shipped. This lent credibility to the company. She placed her order and received an immediate confirmation E-mail that her order had been received. The following day Lori received another E-mail confirming that the order had been shipped.

That day the first company replied to her E-mail; the items she wanted were in stock. It was too late. Lori lost trust in the company when it did not reply in a timely manner. *If a company does not answer its E-mails quickly,* she thought, *how reliable would it be if I ordered?*

Lori was reasonable and patient by giving the first company ample time to answer her E-mail. When it did not respond, she lost faith in the company. Chances are next time Lori needs to order china online, she will choose the company that responded quickly to her needs.

159

LOOKING
BEFORE
YOU LEAP:
E-COMMERCE
CONTACTS

E-commerce Contacts
QUICK QUOTES

Demonstrate you are trustworthy and legitimate

Respond to customers quickly

Show you have a human touch

Take extra care with all your customers

Appreciate every customer

Review E-mail messages before hitting the send button

Never give customers a reason to lose trust in you

In multi-cultural situations, be respectful of differences

Try to see things from your customer's perspective

The customer is the reason you have a job—
that includes your E-customers

CHAPTER 7

Calming the Storm: Difficult Customer Contacts

WHEN A CUSTOMER COMPLAINS,
LOOK AT IT AS AN OPPORTUNITY TO IMPROVE.

Write down a contact in which a customer was upset with your company:

_____

_____

_____

_____

_____

_____

_____

_____

Think about this scenario as you work through this chapter. Use it as the example when answering the practice lesson questions.

You have covered a lot of ground so far. You have learned how to effectively communicate and build relationships with your customers. You have learned special skills to interact with customers face to face, by telephone, and online. You have valuable techniques to effectively handle your customers, but there is still the dreaded difficult customer. A difficult customer can rattle even the most patient, the most composed customer service employee. Learning how to deal with a difficult customer will give you the self-assurance to effectively help each and every one of your customers.

Customers may be difficult to deal with for several reasons. They may be upset because something was mishandled by your company, frustrated about a delay in handling a request, impatient about your company's response time, or maybe they are having a bad day and taking their frustration out on you. Whatever the reason for being difficult, how well you handle each difficult customer can determine whether or not they remain your customers in the future.

 **PICTURE THIS**

Mike is a service representative for an appliance repair company. He has had this job for five years and is experienced in handling customers. Except . . . those who are difficult. Mike does not know how to handle difficult customers, so he usually becomes defensive. When he receives a call from Mr. Roberts, here is what happens.

"ABC Appliance Repair, this is Mike speaking."

"Mike, This is Mr. Roberts. My service contract number is ACH2234. I'm not very happy right now. I called early this morning, and you were supposed to send a service person before noon. Now it's twelve thirty, and no one's showed."

"Hold on," Mike answers with a slight tinge of rudeness in his voice.

"Hold on? I don't want to hold on. My time is valuable, and I don't have all day to wait around. I want to know how soon someone will be out."

163

CALMING
THE STORM:
DIFFICULT
CUSTOMER
CONTACTS

"Mr. Roberts, you need to hold while I check on this for you. We don't make a habit of making appointments we can't keep. We don't normally tell people we'll be out if we don't have someone to send out."

"I'm telling you someone was supposed to be here."

"Just a minute, I'm still checking our records. . . . OK, I see what happened. Looks like when you called this morning we did tell you we could send a person right out, *but you told us you were going to call back to schedule the service call. We have no record that you called us back. I can schedule you for service tomorrow.*"

"I'm not waiting until tomorrow. I told the employee I would call back if I couldn't rearrange my schedule. She told me I was scheduled for this morning. The appointment was set. Tomorrow isn't satisfactory. I want someone out now."

"Evidently you told the rep you were going to call back. That's what she noted on the record. If you had scheduled an appointment when you spoke to her we would have sent someone out."

"I know what was said in our conversation, and I know I was scheduled for service this morning."

"Well, the soonest we can be out is tomorrow."

"Tomorrow isn't satisfactory. I've been sitting home all morning waiting for the service person."

"We don't have service people just sitting here waiting for calls. Everyone has already been dispatched today."

"Obviously I'm not getting through to you. I had an appointment for this morning. The person hasn't arrived. I need a person out this afternoon. Let me speak to a supervisor."

What Went Wrong?

Did Mr. Roberts cause his own problem by saying he would call back?

Did the representative clearly state that she would not make an appointment until he called back?

When Mike received this call, he could not immediately tell what had happened. From what Mr. Roberts had told him, it was clear that there was a miscommunication with the previous representative. Whether Mr. Roberts has a valid reason to be upset should not be important right now. He *is* upset. He has a problem that needs to be dealt with in a manner that is satisfactory to him and suitable to the company. It is Mike's responsibility to handle the problem.

HOW DID THE CUSTOMER FEEL?

Think about this contact from Mr. Roberts' perspective.

What do you think about the manner in which Mike spoke to Mr. Roberts?

_____

_____

_____

_____

How did Mike make Mr. Roberts feel?

_____

_____

_____

_____

What did Mike do right?

_____

_____

_____

_____

What did Mike do wrong?

_____

_____

_____

_____

How effective was Mike in helping Mr. Roberts?

_____

_____

_____

_____

165

CALMING
THE STORM:
DIFFICULT
CUSTOMER
CONTACTS

What do you think Mr. Roberts thinks about the company after this phone call? _____

_____

_____

_____

It is not always easy to know what to say or how to handle customers who are upset from the moment you begin your conversation. However, satisfying a customer who is angry, upset, aggressive, or even rude can be accomplished in any situation. How well you are able to calm difficult customers will make the difference between satisfying them and fostering their feelings of frustration.

Remember the next time a customer complains, there usually is a legitimate reason. Sometimes, though, you will deal with customers who have no basis for their complaints. By learning how to tactfully handle a difficult customer in any situation you can make every customer feel satisfied at the end of the contact.

Master and practice the five-step process and you will arm yourself with the confidence to positively handle any customer in any situation.

> **STEP 1: What Is Going on: Determine the Reason**
> **STEP 2: What Caused It: Identify the Root Cause of the Problem**
> **STEP 3: What Can I Do: Rectify the Situation**
> **STEP 4: What Can I Say: Acknowledge the Problem**
> **STEP 5: What Needs to Be Done: Fix What Needs to Be Fixed**

In the contact with Mr. Roberts, Mike could have done many things differently. Mr. Roberts' perception was that he had an appointment. Mr. Roberts' perception about the situation *is what is important.* Who is right and who is wrong is not important. Making the transition from difficult customer to satisfied customer *is* important.

In answer to the questions, Mike may have said something like:

> *What do you think about the manner in which Mike spoke to Mr. Roberts?*
> *Mike became defensive.*
> *He spoke in a rude tone.*

How did Mike make Mr. Roberts feel?
    He made Mr. Roberts even more upset.

What did Mike do right?
    He was honest when he explained what happened.

What did Mike do wrong?
    He became defensive. He did not appear to listen carefully. He blamed Mr. Roberts for causing the problem.

How effective was Mike in helping Mr. Roberts?
    Not very. Mr. Roberts became even more upset.

What do you think Mr. Roberts thinks about the company after this phone call?
    He is not very happy and certainly not at all satisfied with the way Mike spoke to him.

167

CALMING
THE STORM:
DIFFICULT
CUSTOMER
CONTACTS

STEP 1: What Is Going on: Determine the Reason

The first step is the most critical. What you say, what you do not say, and how you say it are all important. Your customer is upset, and you do not want to do anything to make him more upset.

Assure the customer you are going to help. In your opening statement, tell your customer you will do what you can to resolve the problem. When you give your assurance up front, it can help put your customer in a different frame of mind.

Restate the customer's opening statement. Customers who are upset or angry may not communicate well. They may ramble, raise their voices, and not be able to verbalize what is going on. By restating the opening statement before going any further, you will make sure you are on the right track.

Listen carefully. After assuring the customer you are going to help, listen to the story without interrupting. Listen to the complaint *and* the reason why the customer is being difficult. Mr. Roberts' *complaint* is that the service person was supposed to be dispatched in the morning. His *reason for being difficult* is that he is frustrated because he spent valuable time waiting and no one arrived. By actively listening to *what* the customer is saying rather than *the way* it is said, you will be able to stay focused on providing help. If the customer is having trouble articulating, say something such as, *"Please tell me what happened when you called earlier."*

Write down key details. Pay attention to clues that will help you understand what happened. Make note of things that will help you solve the problem, such as the dates the customer called, what he or she was told by whom, and what actually happened.

Display empathy. Before you proceed, let the customer know that you understand her feelings. Reassure her again that you will help. Try to put yourself in your customer's shoes. No matter how a customer speaks to you, look at the problem from his or her perspective. You will be surprised how much clearer the problem will be when you see the situation from the customer's vantage point rather than your own.

Remain composed. It is important that you stay composed from the beginning of your contact with a difficult customer. A customer speaking angrily or condescendingly may cause you to react in the same manner and tone. Becoming defensive and mirroring a customer's behavior will only agitate the customer further. By maintaining self-control, you will give yourself time to analyze the cause for the customer's anger. When you remain calm, the customer will begin to calm down. You will defuse the fuse.

Remember that a difficult customer is not angry at you personally. Think about this the next time someone is upset or difficult. Even if the customer refers to the company as *you,* as Mr. Roberts did with Mike, and you know *you* personally were not the cause of the problem, remember the customer is not attacking you. The customer sees you as the company. Focus solely on the customer's problem to keep from becoming defensive.

HOW COULD MIKE HAVE HANDLED THE BEGINNING OF THE CONTACT BETTER?

"ABC Appliance Repair, this is Mike speaking."

"Mike, This is Mr. Roberts. My service contract number is ACH2234. I'm not very happy right now. I called early this morning, and you were supposed to send a service person before noon. Now it's twelve thirty and no one's showed."

"Mr. Roberts, I'll be happy to help you. You had a service appointment scheduled for this morning?"

"Yes, that's correct. I called first thing. The employee I spoke with told me she could send someone out this morning. I've been waiting all morning and no one came. I'm a busy person, and my time is valuable. I need someone out right away."

"I understand. I'll need to check our records to see what happened. Can you hold while I do that?"

"Yes, I'll hold."

169

CALMING
THE STORM:
DIFFICULT
CUSTOMER
CONTACTS

Mike assured Mr. Roberts he would resolve his problem. Next he restated Mr. Roberts' opening statement to make sure he understood the problem. Then Mike actively listened and noted that Mr. Roberts was upset because he waited for a service person all morning. He displayed empathy by telling Mr. Roberts he understood and said he would need to check the records. By handling the customer in a calm, unthreatening manner, he displayed confidence to Mr. Roberts that he would resolve the problem.

 If an angry customer immediately asks for your manager or the owner of your company without first giving you a chance to help, try this approach: *"Ms. Customer, please give me the opportunity to resolve the problem. I'm confident that I will be able to help you, but if you are still not satisfied, I will personally refer your problem to my manager (or owner)."* Your confident manner will give the customer the peace of mind that you are truly interested in resolving her problem.

 If a customer uses profanity, calmly say *"Mr. Customer, I understand you are upset, and I am going to help you, but there is no reason to use profanity."* In most cases the customer will stop. If he continues, calmly say, *"I am going to work with you to resolve your problem. Will you please explain to me what happened without using profanity?"* Again, by maintaining a calm demeanor, your customer will begin to calm down.

STEP 2: What Caused It: Identify the Root Cause of the Problem

Once you determine the reason the customer is upset, your next step is to figure out the cause of the problem. In Mr. Roberts' case, Mike should have a clear idea of the complaint. Mr. Roberts called earlier and scheduled a morning appointment. He is upset because it is past noon and no one has been out. Now Mike can figure out what caused the problem.

Investigate the situation. Mike asked Mr. Roberts to hold so he could find out what happened. Mike can check while the customer holds by reviewing the customer's account record and the appointment log. When the investigation will take longer, make a specific commitment to get back to the customer. When making commitments to call back it is important to give a specific time frame rather than telling the customer you will call back *"as soon as possible"* or *"right away."* Terms like these mean different things to different people. Right away might mean sometime today to you—it could mean within fifteen minutes to your customer.

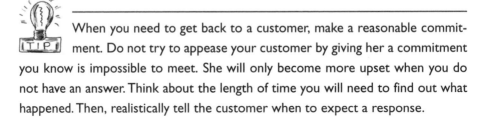

When you need to get back to a customer, make a reasonable commitment. Do not try to appease your customer by giving her a commitment you know is impossible to meet. She will only become more upset when you do not have an answer. Think about the length of time you will need to find out what happened. Then, realistically tell the customer when to expect a response.

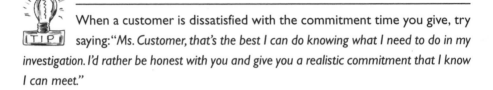

When a customer is dissatisfied with the commitment time you give, try saying: *"Ms. Customer, that's the best I can do knowing what I need to do in my investigation. I'd rather be honest with you and give you a realistic commitment that I know I can meet."*

Determine if the customer has a valid complaint. After investigating, you should be able to figure out whether the customer's complaint is legitimate. Most

171

CALMING
THE STORM:
DIFFICULT
CUSTOMER
CONTACTS

likely it will be. If, after your investigation, you cannot determine what caused the problem, rule in favor of the customer. In Mr. Roberts' situation, Mike is not going to know who caused the miscommunication. From his investigation, he knows the root cause is the misunderstanding that occurred between Mr. Roberts and the first employee. Mike knows that Mr. Roberts expected a service person to be dispatched this morning. He should assume that Mr. Roberts' perception is correct.

Apologize. What is said next is crucial. First, say *"I'm sorry."* It is the right thing to do whether or not your company is at fault. Whenever someone or something causes your customers to be upset, apologizing will let them know you care.

Explain what happened. After you apologize, tell the customer what happened. Stick to the facts. Keep the emotion out of it. Be truthful, even when your company made a mistake. The customer may not like the answer, but your honesty will be appreciated. In the end, a customer is going to respect an employee who is frank and honest over one who evades, covers up, or lies.

HOW COULD MIKE HAVE IDENTIFIED THE ROOT CAUSE OF MR. ROBERTS' PROBLEM?

"Yes, I'll hold."

"Mr. Roberts, thank you for holding. I checked our records, and I apologize that we weren't out this morning. From what I can tell when you spoke to the employee, she was under the assumption that you needed to call back to schedule your appointment. The reason we weren't out is that we didn't hear back from you and therefore never scheduled the service call."

Mike took the time to investigate and determine the root cause. He could not determine whether the customer's complaint was valid since it was the result of a miscommunication. He apologized and stayed neutral when he explained what happened. By staying neutral, Mike is not taking or assigning blame.

What to Do When Customers Do Not Have Valid Complaints

In the event that the customer has no basis for a complaint, you and your manager will need to make a decision whether to appease him or her. Pacifying customers who do not have valid complaints can become costly—only your company knows what price you can pay to keep a customer.

Each case will be different; you will need to decide which customers are worth the effort. What are some situations that may arise in your business where a customer has no basis for her complaint? Think about the following questions, and come up with some guidelines for handling these situations.

→ Is this a one-time complaint or is the customer a chronic complainer?

→ What is your previous relationship with this customer?

→ Does the customer do enough business with your company to make the aggravation worthwhile?

→ Is this person a new customer you want to keep?

There will be occasions when you will need to make the tough decision that it is not cost effective to keep doing business with a customer who requires more than you can afford to satisfy. In these cases, refer to your manager as the one to end the business relationship.

173

CALMING
THE STORM:
DIFFICULT
CUSTOMER
CONTACTS

STEP 3: What Can I Do: Rectify the Situation

You investigated and determined the cause of the problem. Now it is time to offer a solution. If you can rectify the problem to the customer's satisfaction, you get off easy. *"Mr. Roberts, we have a service person who just called in. We're dispatching her to your home, and she'll be there within fifteen minutes."*

How many times does that happen? More than likely the solution you are going to offer is not what the customer wants to hear. How you handle this will make a big difference in what happens next.

Tell the customer what you are going to do to solve the problem. Explain to your customer exactly what you will be able to do to rectify the problem. Take a deep breath before proceeding. Think about what you will say and how you are going to say it.

Focus on what you *can* do. Always focus on the positive of what you can do, rather than on what you cannot do. In the case of Mr. Roberts, all the service people have their schedules for today so sending someone out this afternoon is not an option. What *can* Mike do for him? Before offering the solution, perhaps Mike can check with his dispatcher to see if he can schedule a service call for the first appointment tomorrow morning. While this is not the ideal solution Mr. Roberts is expecting, it does narrow his wait time and gives him preferential treatment.

Offer your best solution. This is not the time to offer something mediocre and begin a bartering session for a better solution. By offering the best you can do, you will be more confident in presenting the solution. Putting yourself in the customer's shoes will help you understand how your solution may be received.

Never assign blame. When you offer your solution, do not fault the customer. For example, how would you feel hearing the following: *"If you had scheduled your appointment the first time you called we would have come out."* Statements like this will put the customer on the defensive. When you are trying to help a difficult customer, blaming serves no purpose. Likewise, never blame another employee or department. Saying, *"The first employee you spoke with should have scheduled your appointment,"* may relieve you from blame, but this statement serves no purpose. To the customer, you are the company. Use *I* or *we* when referring to your company to show you are accountable.

Display empathy. If the customer expresses dissatisfaction, which he very well may do, let him know you understand. Understanding can often help mend broken bridges. You may not be able to fix the problem exactly how he would like but at least you can let him know you understand his feelings and what he is going through.

Offer an alternative solution. If your best solution is not suitable for the customer, try to find something that will work. In the case of Mr. Roberts, perhaps he cannot be home tomorrow morning. Offer a different time frame. If you are at a loss to know how to resolve a problem, ask the customer what she would do to solve the problem if this were her business. Asking that question will help the customer walk in your shoes. Work together to come up with a realistic solution that is mutually acceptable.

HOW COULD MIKE HAVE RECTIFIED THE SITUATION WITH MR. ROBERTS?

"All our service people have already been dispatched for today but here's what I can do for you. I checked with our dispatch department to get you the earliest possible appointment. We can schedule you for the first appointment tomorrow. Someone will be out before nine."

"I want someone out today."

"I understand. If I waited all morning, I'd be upset too. I wish I could change what happened on your first phone call. It looks like there was a mix up in the communication since you thought you were scheduled and the employee thought you had to call back. Unfortunately, all our service people have already been dispatched for today. That's why I checked with my dispatcher to get you the best appointment for tomorrow morning. I know this isn't what you were hoping for, but it's the best I can do and at least you won't have to wait all morning again."

"You say the person will be here before nine?"

"Yes, we already have you set up. I get in at eight tomorrow, and I'll personally follow up on this to make sure nothing goes wrong again."

"Well, Mike, I do appreciate you doing what you can. I guess tomorrow first thing is the best you can do."

"Yes, sir, it is."

175

CALMING
THE STORM:
DIFFICULT
CUSTOMER
CONTACTS

Mike told Mr. Roberts what he was going to do for him. He spoke in a confident manner and focused on what he could do. He checked with his dispatcher before offering the solution. He went a step further to offer preferential treatment for the appointment. Mike let Mr. Roberts know he understood how he felt. Finally, he did not assign blame, either to Mr. Roberts or to the previous employee.

Taking the time to adequately explain your solution will help you communicate more effectively. Tell the customer what you can do, but also explain *why* that is your best solution.

What to Do When the Customer Still Is Not Satisfied

What happens when you cannot resolve the problem to the customer's satisfaction? What if Mr. Roberts still demanded an appointment today?

Discuss situations where you were unable to obtain a satisfactory solution to a customer's problem. How should you handle customers whose requests are impossible to satisfy? Think about the following questions and come up with some guidelines.

→ What alternative solutions can you offer customers?

→ What should you say to customers you cannot satisfy?

→ At what point should you involve your manager (or owner)?

There may be times when, no matter what you offer, you cannot rectify the problem to the customer's satisfaction. When this happens, make sure to communicate that you appreciate the customer's point of view. State that you did your best, there is nothing more you can do, and you are sorry you were not able to work out a satisfactory solution.

STEP 4: What Can I Say: Acknowledge the Problem

What you say next can go a long way in restoring a broken relationship. Just as in a personal relationship, when something damages that bond you have to work hard to rebuild the relationship. The same goes for your business relationships.

Thank the customer for allowing you to make things right. After you satisfactorily resolve a customer's problem, go one step further and say thank you. You cannot take back what happened, but you can do something to let your customer know you value him or her as much as you value the business.

Tell what you will do to avoid future problems. OK, so you solved this customer's problem. What will stop it from happening again? Let your customer know that resolving this problem is important to your company. Then let the customer know what steps you will take to avoid future situations. Positively stating what you will do to fix it will give the customer renewed confidence in your company. When someone takes the time to acknowledge that there is a problem that can be fixed, it makes the customer feel valued. You send the message that your company truly does care about its customers. Plus, your customer will feel he is part of the solution.

Offer some sort of compensation or restitution. When your company is at fault and is the cause of the customer's problem, give the customer something more than is asked for, even if it is only a symbolic gesture. Doing this will not make the problem go away, but it will make the customer feel good about you and your company.

Make a follow-up call or visit. As a courtesy to your customer, follow up to make sure the solution was satisfactory. Think about this: The customer could have taken his business elsewhere without telling you about his dissatisfaction. You would have lost a valued customer. By telling you about a problem, the customer is giving you and your company the opportunity to improve.

177

CALMING
THE STORM:
DIFFICULT
CUSTOMER
CONTACTS

HOW COULD MIKE HAVE ACKNOWLEDGED THE PROBLEM?

"Mr. Roberts, thanks for being so understanding. I don't know what happened on your first phone call, but I am going to refer this to my manager so she can talk to everyone about it. That way, hopefully, we can avoid situations like this in the future."

Next afternoon:

"Mr. Roberts, this is Mike from ABC. I wanted to check back with you and make sure the service person was out this morning and fixed the problem."

"Yes, Mike, she was out first thing and everything is fine now. Thanks for calling me back."

Mike thanked Mr. Roberts for allowing him to fix the problem. He told him what he was going to do to avoid similar problems in the future. The company was not clearly at fault, so Mike did not offer any additional compensation or restitution beyond scheduling the priority appointment. Finally, he made a follow-up call to make sure Mr. Roberts was satisfied. What do you think Mr. Roberts feels about his interaction with this company now?

What to Offer as Compensation and Restitution

Discuss appropriate forms of compensation or restitution to offer customers when your company caused something to go wrong.

What would be the most effective form of compensation for your business? Think about your customers. What would be meaningful to them and appropriate for your type of business? Think, too, about which situations deserve an offer of compensation or restitution. Come up with different scenarios and what you will do. Also discuss who has the authority to approve compensation.

Some examples might be:

→ priority treatment for the next appointment

→ credit toward the service charge or fees rendered

→ a gift certificate or discount toward a future purchase

→ an inexpensive give away, such as a pen, key chain, or logo cap

179

CALMING
THE STORM:
DIFFICULT
CUSTOMER
CONTACTS

STEP 5: What Needs to Be Done: Fix What Needs to Be Fixed

All right, now you have satisfactorily taken care of the customer's problem. But unless you fix what went wrong, the same type of problem is likely to happen again. Do you want to repeatedly deal with difficult customers on the same issue?

Analyze what went wrong. This step is crucial. Sometimes it will not be easy to analyze what went wrong. In Mike's case, all he can determine is that a miscommunication occurred between Mr. Roberts and the previous employee. Although that is as far as the analyzing will go, something can still be done to fix a potential problem. Mike or his supervisor can address the issue in a meeting or by sending a memo to all employees. For example, the manager can ask employees to verify and clarify all appointments (or lack of) before ending the contacts. If the first employee had said, *"Mr. Roberts, I will make a note that you are going to call back to schedule your appointment. I do want to let you know that when you call back there is no guarantee we will still have appointments open for today."* Had that been said, there would not have been a difficult customer.

Review your company's policies and procedures. If you have frequent customer complaints in one area, it is a good idea to look at your policies and procedures. Are there some aspects of your business that customers frequently complain about? It should be your main goal to make it easy for your customers to do business with your company. When it is easy for customers to do business with you, it is easier for you to satisfy them. As a customer service employee, you are in the position to know what makes things difficult for your customers.

Change what you can to make things better. When you are part of the solution, you will be more satisfied with the work you do. Remember, that *you can make a difference.*

 If you cannot easily determine which areas make it difficult for your customers to do business with you, try this. Do a "walk through" of each step of a customer transaction. Look at your company from a customer's perspective. Talk to your manager about the specific ways your company can improve.

How to Fix What Needs Fixing

Discuss any areas that make it difficult for your customers to do business with you. Try to come up with ways to change those areas and rewrite your company's policies to address them. Think about the following questions and come up with some guidelines.

➔ How easy is it for customers to do business with you?

➔ Which of your policies makes it difficult to satisfy your customers?

➔ In what areas of your business do you get repeat complaints?

 **PICTURE THIS**

"ABC Appliance Repair, this is Mike speaking."

"Mike, This is Mr. Roberts. My service contract number is ACH2234. I'm not very happy right now. I called early this morning, and you were supposed to send a service person before noon. Now it's twelve thirty and no one's showed."

"Mr. Roberts, I'll be happy to help you. You had a service appointment scheduled for this morning?"

"Yes, that's correct. I called first thing. The employee I spoke with told me she could send someone out this morning. I've been waiting all morning and no one came. I'm a busy person, and my time is valuable. I need someone out right away."

"I understand. I'll need to check our records to see what happened. Can you hold while I do that?"

"Yes, I'll hold."

"Mr. Roberts, thank you for holding. I checked our records and I apologize that we weren't out this morning. From what I can tell when you spoke to the employee, she was under the assumption that you

181

CALMING
THE STORM:
DIFFICULT
CUSTOMER
CONTACTS

needed to call back to schedule your appointment. The reason we weren't out is that we didn't hear back from you and, therefore, never scheduled the service call.

"All our service people have already been dispatched for today, but here's what I can do for you. I checked with our dispatch department to get you the earliest possible appointment. We can schedule you for the first appointment tomorrow. Someone will be out before nine."

"I want someone out today."

"I understand. If I waited all morning, I'd be upset too. I wish I could change what happened on your first phone call. It looks like there was a mix up in the communication since you thought you were scheduled and the employee thought you had to call back. Unfortunately, all our service people have already been dispatched for today. That's why I checked with my dispatcher to get you the best appointment for tomorrow morning. I know this isn't what you were hoping for, but it's the best I can do and at least you won't have to wait all morning again."

"You say the person will be here before nine?"

"Yes, we already have you set up. I get in at eight tomorrow, and I'll personally follow up on this to make sure nothing goes wrong again."

"Well, Mike, I do appreciate you doing what you can. I guess tomorrow first thing is the best you can do."

"Yes, sir, it is. Thanks for being so understanding. I don't know what happened on your first phone call, but I am going to refer this to my manager so she can talk to everyone about it. That way, hopefully, we can avoid situations like this in the future."

Next afternoon:

"Mr. Roberts, this is Mike from ABC. I wanted to check back with you and make sure the service person was out this morning and fixed the problem."

"Yes, Mike, she was out first thing and everything is fine now. Thanks for calling me back."

All your difficult customers will not be as easy to satisfy as Mr. Roberts, but if you master the steps for handling difficult customers you will gain the confidence to positively handle any of them. When you have confidence in your ability, it will reflect back to your customers. When you are confident in yourself, customers will be confident in your ability to do your best for them.

The bottom line is that when you deal with customers, there *are* going to be problems. Whether the problem is caused by the customer or by the company, what is important in any contact with a difficult customer is what you do to resolve the problem and how valued you make the customer feel.

MAKE SURE YOUR ATTITUDE IS NEVER *INDIFFERENT*
BUT ALWAYS INTERESTED *IN MAKING A DIFFERENCE.*

183

CALMING
THE STORM:
DIFFICULT
CUSTOMER
CONTACTS

Difficult Customer Contacts
KEY POINTS

STEP 1: What Is Going on: Determine the Reason

Assure the customer you are going to help

Restate the customer's opening statement

Listen carefully

Write down key details

Display empathy

Remain composed

STEP2: What Caused It: Identify the Root Cause of the Problem

Investigate the situation

Determine if the customer has a valid complaint

Apologize

Explain what happened

STEP 3: What Can I Do: Rectify the Situation

Tell the customer what you are going to do to solve the problem

Focus on what you *can* do

Offer your best solution

Never assign blame

Display empathy

Offer an alternative solution

STEP 4: What Can I Say: Acknowledge the Problem

Thank the customer for allowing you to make things right

Tell the customer what you will do to avoid future problems

Offer some sort of compensation or restitution

Make a follow up call or visit

STEP 5: What Needs to Be Done: Fix What Needs to Be Fixed

Analyze what went wrong

Review company policies and procedures

Change what you can to make things better

Difficult Customer Contacts
PRACTICE LESSON

Refer to the customer contact example you noted at the beginning of the chapter.

STEP 1: What Is Going on: Determine the Reason
Write down the customer's opening statement.

_____

_____

_____

_____

Write a statement assuring this customer you are going to help. Restate the customer's opening statement to ensure your understanding

_____

_____

_____

_____

How will you display empathy to let the customer know you understand?

_____

_____

_____

_____

STEP 2: What Caused It: Identify the Root Cause of the Problem
After investigating the situation, determine if the customer has a valid complaint. Need more time to investigate? Assume you are going to need to research further and you will need to call the customer back. Write an example of how you will state the commitment.

_____

_____

_____

_____

185

CALMING
THE STORM:
DIFFICULT
CUSTOMER
CONTACTS

Write a statement explaining what happened.

_____

_____

_____

_____

STEP 3: What Can I Do: Rectify the Situation

Write a statement telling the customer what you can do to solve the problem.

_____

_____

_____

_____

If the customer objects, write a statement offering empathy.

_____

_____

_____

_____

Assume this customer is not satisfied with your resolution. Write an alternate solution you could offer.

_____

_____

_____

_____

STEP 4: What Can I Say: Acknowledge the Problem

Write a statement thanking the customer for allowing you to correct the problem.

_____

_____

_____

_____

Tell the customer what you will do to avoid future problems.

_____

_____

_____

_____

Was this problem caused by your company? Remember to leave your customer with a good impression of you and your business by offering some sort of compensation or restitution. What will you offer this customer?

_____

_____

_____

_____

What will you say to the customer in your follow up call?

_____

_____

_____

_____

STEP 5: What Needs to Be Done: Fix What Needs to Be Fixed
Think about this situation. Analyze what went wrong. What can you and your company do to avoid similar problems in the future? Write out what changes you will make.

_____

_____

_____

_____

Remember, the important thing to keep in mind is to always strive to make it easy for your customers to do business with you.

187

CALMING
THE STORM:
DIFFICULT
CUSTOMER
CONTACTS

Think About . . .

Have **you** ever caused a customer to be difficult?

Sharon contacted a company she deals with on a regular basis to place an order. The representative asked for her account number. After giving it to him, he promptly told her it was the wrong number. She verified the number she has used for years. Again, she was told, bluntly, that it was wrong.

"This is the number I've always used," Sharon assured him.

"Well," he responded in a condescending voice, "you must be wrong. All our account numbers begin with a letter and yours doesn't."

Sharon was not happy with the way she was being treated so she answered in an equally condescending voice, "This *is* my account number. In fact, I called last month and used it."

"I don't know what to tell you," he again explained, becoming rude as he re-stated his position. "That isn't one of our account numbers."

His attitude caused Sharon to become a difficult customer. She had been a customer of this company for years. She was not going to accept this treatment. She asked for a supervisor. The supervisor she spoke to immediately explained the problem. The company had recently changed their account numbers. Sharon was using the old account number, but since she was a long time customer, the supervisor assured her they could access her account by cross-referencing it in their system.

Even if the representative was not aware of the cross-reference procedure, had he remained courteous to Sharon she would not have become a difficult customer. There was no reason for him to handle the contact that way.

IN ANY CONTACT WITH ANY CUSTOMER, HOW YOU SPEAK AND THE TONE YOU USE CAN TURN A PLEASANT CUSTOMER INTO A DIFFICULT ONE— FOR NO REASON.

Difficult Customer Contacts
QUICK QUOTES

Put yourself in the customers' shoes and try to see things
from their perspective

The customer is not angry at you personally

Focus on the problem, not the person's attitude or behavior

Display empathy towards the customer's situation

Think about what you can do

Be part of the solution

Take pride in turning an upset customer into a satisfied one

Never interrupt when customers are telling their side of things

It is all right to ask for the customer's ideas for solutions

Feel proud when you can turn an upset customer into a satisfied one

PART III

Putting It All Together

CHAPTER 8

Hitting the Ground Running: Ready, Set, Go

BEING GOOD AT WHAT YOU DO
MAKES DOING IT A PLEASURE.

You have covered a lot of ground in this book. Part I focused on putting your best face forward. You have learned how to present yourself by using basic courtesies, communicating effectively, and building strong relationships. Part II focused on putting your customers first. You learned special skills to handle customers—even difficult customers—in person, on the telephone, and through the Internet. Now, it is time to put it all together. You are on your way to giving great customer service. Where do you go from here?

Before proceeding, review your list of learning outcomes. Do you feel confident that you can apply the lessons you learned to each item on your list? If you are not sure about any of the items, review the relevant chapters again. Go back over any sections of the training material until you feel comfortable applying the material to your customer situations. If you still feel uncomfortable with any of the items, talk them over with your manager. To get the most out of this training, it is important that you feel confident with the total package.

Are you ready to hit the ground running? Not everyone will be ready for that huge step. Depending on your comfort level, you may either be ready to jump in with both feet, you may be ready to toss the ball back and forth, or you may only be ready to take your first baby steps. If you feel comfortable and confident, go ahead and run with this material. But, if you feel a little overwhelmed by all that you learned, don't worry. Begin with baby steps. In fact, even if you are confident that you are ready to apply everything you learned, it might be a good idea for you to focus on one area at a time so that you can turn each of these lessons into lifelong habits.

Start with the basics. Focus on the way you present yourself when people are forming their first impressions of you. Get used to using the courtesy words and phrases: please, thank you, excuse me, I'm sorry, yes, and so on. When you find yourself using these words without thinking, pay attention to your attitude. Remember that your attitude includes how you talk to yourself. Make it a habit to use positive words in your self-talk. Make it a habit to always act in an ethical manner.

When you are comfortable with the basics, focus on communicating effectively. Think before you speak so you will say what you mean and mean what you say. Pay attention to the nonverbal messages you send by being aware of your body language. You are on your way to presenting yourself well. Next, focus on your questioning skills. It may help to write down some sample open and closed questions that you will frequently use. Review them often so you will become comfortable using them. Remember that no matter what type of question a customer asks you, always try to give more than a one word answer. Give your customers more than they ask for. When customers say no, find out the reason and do the right thing based on each customer's needs. Finally, and most importantly, listen actively. As your company's communicator, listening is your most important job when you communicate with customers. Unless you listen well, you are not going to know exactly what is best for your customers.

At this point you are ready to form strong relationships with your customers. You have learned the nuts and bolts of communicating effectively; now it is time to add some pizzazz to your customer contacts. Let your personality shine. Establish a rapport by being friendly and interested in your customers so you can find common ground. Once you establish a rapport, you will find it easy to interact positively with your customers. You learned how to develop a comfort level with your customers and will be able to help each customer by identifying individual needs. When you do these things, you will make your customers feel valued. When customers feel valued, they are more likely to do repeat business with you and your company. The last thing you learned about relationships is that not all customers are the same. You learned how to deal with different personality types, people from different cultures, and people with disabilities. The most important thing to remember is to treat all your customers the way you like to be treated.

Practice each of these steps. Each one is a building block you firmly cement on your customer service foundation. By the time you are comfortable using all the principles learned in Part I, you have built a strong foundation. The more you use the principles, the more comfortable and confident you will be when you apply them to the various types of customer contacts you learned in Part II.

Review these steps frequently. It is easy to forget or fall back into old habits. Make a conscious effort to practice these principles every day. Practice using them, not only at work, but also in your interactions with family and friends. Practice using them in situations in which you are the customer. Learning how to communicate well will help you build positive relationships in all areas of your life.

Refer to the list on the next page frequently to make sure you remember to follow all the lessons you learned.

Customer Service Training Quick Reference

The Basics
First impressions matter
Courtesy counts
Attitude is everything
Do the right thing at all times

Effective Communication
Say what you mean and mean what you say
Pay attention to your body language
Use correct grammar
Ask the correct questions and answer the questions correctly
When the customer says no, find out why
Listen actively

Relationship Building
Establish a rapport
Interact positively with customers
Identify customers' needs
Make customers feel valued
Maintain ongoing relationships

Face-to-Face Contacts
Greet the customer
Help the customer
End the transaction by thanking the customer

Telephone Contacts
Listen completely
Greet the customer
Help the customer
End the call by thanking the customer

E-Commerce Contacts

The E-customer is looking for legitimacy, trust, and a human touch

Be accessible

Write carefully so that you write what you intend

When speaking around the world, be mindful of cross-cultural etiquette

Difficult Customer Contacts

Determine the reason the customer is being difficult

Identify the root cause of the problem

Rectify the situation

Acknowledge the problem

Fix what needs to be fixed

CHAPTER 9

Being the Best You Can Be: The Total Package

**MAKE YOURSELF THE
BEST PRODUCT OUT THERE.**

Ready, set? Before you go, there is just one more thing to cover. You read an entire book devoted to helping you give exceptional customer service. This last chapter is devoted to you—only you—to help you be the best you can be in everything you do.

When you focus on being the best person you can be every day, good things will happen to you. People will notice. You may get that promotion for which

you have been hoping. You may get that award for outstanding performance. Even if you do not reap external rewards, internally you will feel good about yourself. You will find increased job satisfaction when you give your best.

Be your best in everything you do, and you will find that you perform better at work, that you give more of yourself to other people, and that you get more happiness and satisfaction in everything you do.

How do you begin being your best?

Take responsibility for your actions. Remember, there is only one person in charge of you. You are in charge of you. You control your actions. You control your performance at work. You control your behavior. You make the decisions for yourself. When you make the decision to be your best at all times, you will strive to achieve your best. You will feel good about the choices you make. You will feel good about yourself. When you feel good about yourself, you will reflect those feelings outward.

Be the person you want to be. Create in your mind a positive vision of the person you want to become. If you have trouble seeing clearly, take time alone to focus on the qualities you want to personify and to envision the "you" you want to be. Keep this vision in your conscious. Change your self-talk to reflect the new you. If your vision is to be more confident and self-assured, act the part. Tell yourself that you are confident and self-assured. Initially it will be difficult and awkward but the more you practice the easier it will become until one day your confident behavior will be second nature and you will no longer be acting.

Set goals for yourself. What will it take for you to become the person you envision yourself being? Do you need to go back to school? Do you need to join an organization that fosters the qualities you wish to exemplify? Write down specific goals. There is something magical about writing your goals on paper. Once they are written, you will become more focused on finding ways to achieve them. If some of your goals are too big or long range, break them into smaller, more manageable goals.

Keep looking forward. It is easy to get mired in the day-to-day grind. It is also easy to get mired in dwelling on the past. When you keep looking forward, it is easier to continue focusing on your goals. Here is where your self-talk is important. You cannot change what happened, but the next time you can do things differently. Change your self-talk to words that will help you move toward your goals. Learn to respect yourself by being respectful of the way you talk to yourself.

Measure your own level of performance. Periodically, answer these questions. Do you feel good, both physically and mentally? Are you happy, both in your job and in your life? Do you look forward to each day, going to work and doing other activities? Are you proud of your efforts? If you answered yes, you are most likely performing well at work and working towards achieving your goals. If you answered no, it is time for self-reflection. Look inward to figure out what is happening and how you can improve yourself and your situation. This might mean rethinking your goals. It may be time to create a more realistic vision of your future so you can set goals that are reachable.

Keep striving. To be your best means to keep striving to be even better. Learn the skills of your job well. Ask questions to learn more. Try to learn something new everyday. Learn from all of your experiences. When something bad happens, learn from it. Do not repeat the same mistake twice. Ask for advice when you need help. Try to anticipate problems before they get out of hand. Be part of the solution, rather than part of the problem. Give your all in everything you do. Take the extra step for your customers, your family, and your friends.

Be a good listener. This theme has been stressed throughout the book, but it cannot be stressed enough. Listening completely is important, not only in work situations, but in every life situation. A good listener equates to a good communicator. When you listen well you become well informed. You learn more. You tune in to others. Learn to listen more than you speak. Speak when you have something meaningful—and constructive—to say. Remember always to think before you speak.

Enjoy and have fun. Being the best you can be has a positive reward: You begin enjoying everything you do. Be positive. Find the good in others. When you encounter someone who is difficult to deal with, whether it is your customer, friend, or significant other, do whatever you can to make that person's day better. When you encounter someone who needs help, feel happy that you *can* help. When you encounter a stranger, smile. Be grateful that you have this day. Be appreciative of those around you. Laugh often. Be happy. Make it a goal to have fun every day.

ALWAYS BE YOUR BEST!

Being the Best You Can Be
QUICK QUOTES

Give each day 110%

Be accountable for your actions

Being good at what you do makes doing it a pleasure

Learn from your experiences—good or bad

Be part of the solution, not part of the problem

Try to come up with better ways to do things

Set performance goals for yourself

Take pride in everything you do

Make yourself the best product out there

Have fun at your job

Being the best you can be shows that you have character.

CHARACTER HAS HEART

The character of a person is found deep in the heart

Be **H**onest	Tell the truth. Do the right thing. Be trustworthy.
Be **E**mpathetic	Put yourself in the other person's shoes. Listen. Care.
Be **A**ppreciative	Look for the good in people. Express gratitude.
Be **R**espectful	Show care, concern, and consideration.
Be **T**olerant	Rather than judging others, accept their differences.

Index

A

accountability, 34

Angry customers. *See* Problem situations

Appreciation, learning, 30

Attitude, 30-32

  and first impression, 22-23

  and self-image, 30

B

Belief in self, 30

Blame, avoiding, 173

Body language. *See* Nonverbal
  communication

C

Character, good, traits of, 201

Cigarette smoking, avoiding, 29

Classroom, choosing training room, 8

Closed questions, 55

Closing

  e-mail, 152

  face-to-face meeting, 113-114

  telephone calls, 134-136

Clothing, and first impression, 26-27

Common ground, and rapport building,
  79

Communication, 43-69

  conveying meaning through, 48-49

  e-mail, 4

  in e-mail, 151

  functions of, 43

  grammatical correctness, 44, 52-53

  key points, 63-64

  listening, 46, 60-62

  nonverbal, 44-45, 50-51

  and objections of customer, 58-59, 83-
    84

  with person of another culture, 49

  practice lesson, 65-66

  professional versus personal, 48-49

  questioning customer, 45, 54-57

  and rapport building, 78-80

  and relationship building, 71-100

  rep as company communicator, 43-44,
    52

  speaking clearly, 52

  tone of voice, 44, 48

  welcome words, 48

Compensating customers, for problem
    situations, 176-178

Competition, avoiding negativity toward,
    34

Courtesy

  end of interaction, 113-114

  and first impression, 22-23

  words/phrases to use, 28-29, 109

Credibility, 81

Culturally-different customers

  communication and culture, 49

  e-mail etiquette, 154

  tolerance for, 89-90

Customer personality differences, 73, 89-
    93

  flirty customer, 89

  pushy customer, 89

  timid customer, 89

Customer service basics, 22-36

  attitude, 22-23, 30-32

  courtesy, 22, 28-29

  ethical issues, 33-36

Customer service basics (*continued*)
    first impression, 22, 26-27
    keypoints, 37
    practice lesson, 38
Customer service training
    importance of, 11-13, 21-22
    learning outcomes, establishing, 13
    preparation for, 14

E
Eating while working, avoiding, 29
E-commerce contacts, 143-159
    credibility of business, 147-149
    key points, 155
    order processing speed, 149
    practice lesson, 156-157
    Web site design, 145-146
    See also E-mail
E-mail
    benefits of, 4
    content, 151-153
    cross-cultural etiquette, 154
    customer name in, 151-152
    grammatical correctness, 154
    mistakes in e-mail, 144-145
    to present customers, 149-150
Emotional baggage, 31
Empathy, in problem situation, 167, 169,
    174
End of service
    closing telephone contact, 134-136
    ending interaction, 113-114
Energy level, maintaining, 51
Ethical issues
    e-commerce, 147
    and rapport building, 79
    types of, 33-36
    unethical behavior, actions to take, 35
Eye contact
    at end of session, 110

    and first impression, 27
    and listening, 60
    as nonverbal message, 45, 50, 61
    with persons with disabilities, 90-91

F
Face-to-face contact, 103-120
    and customer impression, 104-105
    ending interaction, 113-114
    greeting customer, 109-110
    helping stage, 111-112
    and image/look of business, 106-108
    key points, 117
    practice lesson, 118
First impression, 22, 26-27
    and appearance/attire, 26-27
    and attitude, 22-23
    and body language, 27
    and courtesy, 22-23
    and face-to-face contact, 104-105
    opening statement, 109
    and relationship building, 72
    and telephone contact, 128-129
    unfavorable, examples of, 23-25
    wrong, stereotype-based, 39-40
Flirty customers, 89
Follow-up, to problem situations, 176
Friendliness
    and rapport building, 78-80
    and relationship building, 74-75

G
Goal-setting, for self, 198
Grammar, correct and communication,
    44, 52-53, 154
Greeting customers
    face-to-face, 109-110
    telephone contact, 124-125
Grooming, and first impression, 26-27
Gum chewing, avoiding, 29

H

Honesty
  as ethical issue, 33
  and rapport building, 79

I

"I can't," avoiding use, 33, 56
Instructor-led training, elements of, 5

J

Jargon, avoiding, 52

L

Learning outcomes
  areas for improvement, 13
  identifying, 4
Listening, 60-62
  active listening, 60-62
  as communication method, 46, 60
  to customer objections, 58
  nonverbal component, 60-61, 110
  one customer only, 111
  to problem situation, 167-169
  telephone contacts, 124-127

M

Multicultural aspects. *See* Culturally-
  different customers

N

Names of customers
  in e-mail, 151-152
  and relationship building, 87
  telephone contact, 127-128, 134
  use as courtesy, 28
Needs of customers, identifying, 83-84
Negative statements, avoiding, 34
Negative thoughts, positive self-talk for, 30
Nonverbal communication
  clothing/appearance, 26-27

communicating channels of, 44-45,
  110
eye contact, 45, 50, 61
and first impression, 27
while listening, 60-61
posture, 50
smiling, 50
See also specific gestures

O

Objections of customers
  handling of, 58-59, 83-84
  See also Problem situations
Objectivity, and listening, 60-61
Open questions, 54-55

P

Personality types. *See* Customer
  personality differences
Persons with disabilities, interaction
  with, 90-91
Physical appearance
  clothing/grooming, 26-27
  image/look of business, 106-108
Positive interactions
  and customer decisions, 85
  self-talk for, 30
  types of, 81-82
Posture, as nonverbal communication,
  50
Practicing, for training sessions, 7
Praise, as motivator, 9
Preferences of customers, remembering,
  87
Problem situations, 161-188
  acknowledge problem, 176-177
  compensation, offering to customer,
    176-178
  customer remains unsatisfied, 175
  defining problem situation, 167-168

Problem situations (*continued*)
    empathy, communicating, 167, 169, 174
    invalid customer complaints, handling, 172
    investigating problem, 170-172
    key points, 183
    and miscommunication, 163
    multiple-complaints, same issue, 179-182
    practice lesson, 184-186
    problem-solving, 173-175
    solving problem, 179-182
Problem-solving
    customer need for, 83
    and end of interaction, 113
    as positive interaction, 81
    in problem situation, 173-175
Profanity, customer use of, 169
Pushy customers, 89

Q

Questioning customers, 45, 54-57
    answering questions, 55-56
    to control conversation, 55
    and customer objections, 58
    for more information, 54-55
    simplicity in, 54
    "why" questions, cautions about, 55

R

Rapport with customers, 78-80
    and friendliness, 78-80
    and initial communication, 78
    showing interest, 78-79
Relationship building, 71-100
    culturally different customer, 89-90
    customer needs, identifying, 83-84
    and friendliness, 74-75
    importance of, 71-72, 74
    key points, 94-95

    and personality types, 73, 89-93
    and positive interactions, 81-82
    practice lesson, 96-98
    process of, 72-73, 75-76
    rapport, establishing, 78-80
    and repeat customer, 73-74, 87-88
    value of customer, communicating, 85-86
Repeat customers
    e-mails to, 150
    relationship building tips, 73-74, 87-88
    taking for granted, 24

S

Salutation, in e-mail, 151
Schedule, for training sessions, 6-7
Self-control, in problem situation, 168
Self-esteem, belief in self, 30
Self-improvement, steps toward, 197-199
Self-paced training, elements of, 5-6
Self-talk, to learn appreciation, 30
Sensitivity, and rapport building, 79
Showing items, versus directing to, 111
Slang, avoiding, 52
Sleep/rest, importance of, 51
Smiling
    at end of session, 110
    importance of, 29
    as nonverbal message, 29, 50
Stereotyping
    avoiding, 31
    first impression based on, 39-40
Stress management, lifestyle tips, 31, 51

T

Teaching method
    instructor-led training, 5
    planning, 4-5
    self-paced training, 5-6
Technical words, avoiding, 52

Telephone calls, while helping customer, 111
Telephone contacts, 121-141
    closing call, 134-136
    helping stage, 130-133
    hold, putting customer on, 131-132
    interrupting, avoiding, 126
    key points, 137
    listening, 124-127
    name of customer, using, 127-128, 134
    opener, 124-125
    opening call, 128-129
    outgoing phone contacts, 132
    practice lesson, 138-139
Thanking customers, ending interaction, 113-114
Timid customers, 89
Tone of voice, 44, 48

Training needs, identifying, 3-4
Training sessions
    follow-up to, 8-9
    practicing presentations, 7
    room for, 8
    time frame/schedule for, 6-7

V
Value of customers, communicating, 85-86
Visual interest, e-mail messages, 151

W
Web site design, 145-146
    naming company, 148
    See also E-commerce contacts
Welcome words, 48
"Why" questions, 55

Learn More About Additional Titles from AMACOM at www.amacombooks.org

---

Delivering Knock Your Socks Off Service, 3rd Edition by Performance Research Associates $18.95

Great Customer Service on the Telephone by Kristin Anderson $10.95

Laugh and Learn: 96 Ways to Use Humor for More Effective Teaching and Training by Doni Tamblyn $25.00

People Strategies for Trainers: 161 Tips and Techniques for Dealing with Difficult Classroom Situations by Robert W. Lucas $21.95

Quick Team-Building Activities for Busy Managers: 50 Exercises That Get Results in Just 15 Minutes by Brian Cole Miller $17.95

Secret Service: Hidden Systems That Deliver Unforgettable Customer Service by John R. DiJulius III $17.95

Show Biz Training: Fun and Effective Training Techniques from the Worlds of Stage, Screen, and Song by Lenn Millbower $34.95

The AMA Trainers Activity Book: A Selection of the Best Learning Exercises from the World's Premier Training Organization by Carolyn Nilson $39.95

The Conflict and Communication Activity Book: 30 High Impact Training Exercises for Adult Learners by Bill Withers and Keami D. Lewis $34.95

The Emotional Intelligence Activity Book: 50 Activities for Promoting EQ at Work by Adele Lynn $34.95

The EQ Difference: A Powerful Plan for Putting Emotional Intelligence to Work by Adele B. Lynn $16.00

The Leadership Training Activity Book: 50 Exercises for Building Effective Leaders by Lois B. Hart and Charlotte S. Waisman $34.95

Available at your local bookstore, online, or by calling 800-250-5308

Savings start at 35% on **Bulk Orders** of 5 copies or more!
Save up to 55%!
For details, contact AMACOM Special Sales
Phone: 212-903-8316. E-mail: SpecialSls@amanet.org